BY DESIGN, NOT BY CHANCE

There Is Still an Elohim in Yahshar'el Who Fights for His Children

A Testimony of Covenant Protection, Supernatural Provision, and Divine Purpose

By John Alan Legette, B.S. Architectural Studies, B.Arch., M.B.A.

EPIGRAPH PAGE

"Not by might, nor by power, but by My Ruach, says Yahuah of hosts."

— Zechariah 4:6

BY DESIGN, NOT BY CHANCE

There Is Still an Elohim in Yahshar'el Who Fights for His Children

Copyright © 2026 by John Alan Legette

Published by J.A.L.M. Publishing, LLC

Scripture quotations are taken from multiple translations and have been rendered using the sacred names Yahuah and Yahshua HaMashaich in accordance with the author's Hebrew Roots faith tradition and commitment to the restoration of the original covenant names throughout the text.

First Edition, 2026

Printed and distributed worldwide

For permission requests or ministry inquiries, contact J.A.L.M. Publishing, LLC

ISBN (Paperback): 979-8-9930127-3-5

DEDICATION PAGE

To my wife Alexandria — who walked every ascending mile of this journey beside me.

To every believer in their 13th year of homelessness who cannot yet see the blueprint.

To every vessel in their 18th year of drought who does not yet know that the pressing is producing what is about to pour.

To every stone the builders have rejected — He was shaping you for the apex the entire time.

And to Yahuah — the Master Architect who held the blueprint before the foundation of the world and has never revised a single line of it.

This is Your testimony. I am only the vessel.

FOREWORD

By Design, Not By Chance

Foreword

Opening Epigraph

"Neither do men put new wine into old bottles: else the bottles break, and the wine runneth out, and the bottles perish: but they put new wine into new bottles, and both are preserved." — Matthew 9:17

"Behold, I will do a new thing; now it shall spring forth; shall ye not know it? I will even make a way in the wilderness, and rivers in the desert." — Isaiah 43:19

Before You Read This Book

There is one sentence that unlocks every chapter of this testimony.

It is not a sentence I constructed. It is a sentence Yahshua spoke in Matthew 9:17, in response to a question about fasting and new practices and why His disciples did not follow the religious conventions of the moment. His answer reached far beyond the immediate question and landed on a principle that governs the entire economy of how Yahuah prepares vessels for the new things He intends to release through them.

You cannot pour new wine into an old vessel.

If you read this book without that sentence in your hand, you will encounter a series of painful seasons — a drought, a homelessness, a displacement, a home invasion, a pursuit across state lines — and you may be tempted to read those seasons as evidence of abandonment, as the cost of choices poorly made, as the collateral damage of a life lived in difficult circumstances. You may feel the weight of the suffering without understanding its function. You may see the pressure without recognizing the purpose.

But if you read this book with that sentence in your hand, you will encounter something entirely different. You will encounter the systematic, sovereign, architecturally precise work of a Potter who knew exactly what He was making, who never confused the vessel with the wine, who never mistook the kiln for the destination, and who kept the vessel in the fire for exactly as long as the vessel needed to be there — not one day longer, not one day less — before pouring in what He had been preparing to pour in since before the vessel was formed.

The drought was the kiln. The homelessness was the firing. The displacement was the final heat. The pursuit was the pressure test. And the new wine — 82 albums, 1,180 tracks, 589 teachings, 8 books, and the testimony you are now holding — is what flows when a finished vessel receives what it was built to carry.

You cannot pour new wine into an old vessel. Everything in this book is the evidence of that truth being worked out across one man's life in real time, at specific elevations, across ten states, through sixteen weeks of an unplanned evangelical tour that began the morning after a home invasion in Chicago and ended at the apex of an arch that Yahuah had been building since before the author's formation.

What the Old Vessel Was

I was born Jackie Legette II. The second bearing of my father's name. The namesake of a man who was, by any standard I have encountered in my life, a genius — a Seer, a biblical scholar, a man of anointed intelligence who could perceive the spiritual realm with a clarity most people never experience. My father was brilliant in the way that transcends secular knowledge and enters the territory of Spirit-illuminated understanding. He was the most brilliant man I have ever known.

He was also, by his own choices, a man who could not build the house.

Like David — genuinely loved by Yahuah, genuinely gifted, genuinely called — my father was disqualified from the specific assignment that his gifts were pointing toward, because the pattern of his life did not align with the requirements of the building. He used his gifts for his own advancement. He chose his own glory over the glory of the One who gave him the gifts. He had reverence for the Word of Yahuah — deep, genuine reverence — but reverence without full surrender is not covenant faithfulness. And the house cannot be built by a vessel that reserves any portion of itself from the Potter's hand.

My father's potential went largely into the grave with him. And I, as Jackie Legette II — the second bearing of his name, the continuation of his identity, the son who carried both the favor and the cracks of the inherited legacy — was the old vessel. Not because I was unworthy. Not because Yahuah had not placed gifts in me. But because the cracks of the inherited pattern ran through the container, and the new wine that Yahuah intended to pour through me could not be released into an old vessel without running out through those cracks onto the floor of self-glorification and wasted potential.

The Potter did not patch the old vessel. He made a new one.

On December 8, 2016, at 38 years old, Yahuah instructed me to change my name. Jackie Legette II was set aside. John Alan Legette — Noble ambassador favored by Elohim — was inaugurated. The new vessel was placed in the kiln.

Eight years later, at age 46, the kiln work was complete.

And Yahuah poured in the new wine.

What the New Wine Is

In July 2025, at 46 years of age, I produced my first song. I had never produced music before in my life. I do not play instruments. I have no music training, no music background, no music education of any kind. I was a trained architect, a writer, a graphic designer — none of which has any structural relationship to music production. I sat down to hear one song I had written set to sound, and Yahuah gave me an album. I released that album globally on July 31, 2025, and the albums have not stopped coming since.

Eighty-two albums in eight months. One thousand one hundred and eighty tracks. Five hundred and eighty-nine YouTube teachings. Eight books — including this one — none of which existed before 2025, because I had never written a full-length book before in my life either. All of it produced while homeless. All of it produced while being pursued across state lines by people who invested heavily in ensuring it would never exist. All of it produced at a level of quality and volume that caused investigators to travel to my hometown in South Carolina and ask my family and friends whether they had ever known me to make music. They had no answer. They said what the parents of the blind man said in John 9: he is of age, ask him.

My answer is the same answer the blind man gave: one thing I know. Whereas I could not do this before, now I can. I cannot explain the mechanism within the natural order. I can only point to the sentence and tell you it is true.

You cannot pour new wine into an old vessel. But when the vessel is new — when the kiln work is finished and the transformation is complete and the Potter determines the vessel is ready — the wine does not trickle. It floods.

What the Tour Was

On December 10, 2025, our home was invaded. We were driven from Chicago. The people who did this believed they were stopping the testimony. They were completing the kiln.

On December 11, 2025, we went to O'Hare Airport. We caught a flight. The unplanned evangelical tour of the American West began. Over the following sixteen weeks we drove approximately ten thousand to twenty thousand miles through ten states, following the direction of the Ruach without a human itinerary, at elevations that ascended from the Pacific coast at sea level to the Colorado Rockies at 9,280 feet — from the lowest point to the highest, in a sequence no human travel agent arranged, because the architect who designed the sequence had written it into the book before the first step was taken.

Fifty-two albums in the first three months of that tour. Produced while homeless. Produced while being pursued. Produced at accelerating rates at increasing elevations, in a pattern that documents with statistical precision that the output of a surrendered vessel increases in direct proportion to the altitude at which it operates — the higher the climb, the greater the flow.

The tour was not an escape from the opposition. The tour was the new wine being poured out across the American West in real time, filling every location the Ruach designated with the sound of the sacred names Yahuah and Yahshua proclaimed by a man who, five years earlier, had never produced a note of music in his life and who, five months into the tour, had produced more Hebrew Roots music than most full ministries produce in a decade.

The old vessel could not have survived this tour. The old vessel would have broken under the pressure of homelessness, pursuit, and the sustained creative output that the Ruach was requiring. The new vessel — fired in the kiln for 8 years, proven through drought and displacement and opposition, completed at age 46 when the gift arrived that announced the preparation was finished — the new vessel held. The wine ran over. And the testimony you are now holding is the documented overflow.

What This Book Will Do to You

I did not write this book to impress you. I wrote it because someone reading these words right now is in the kiln and does not know it.

You are in a season that feels like abandonment and is actually preparation. You are carrying gifts that feel suppressed and are actually being stored. You are in a drought that feels like failure and is actually compression. You are the vessel being formed for wine you cannot yet imagine, being fired at temperatures you did not choose, being shaped by a Potter whose hands you cannot always feel but who has never for one moment taken His eyes off what He is making.

And the question you are asking — the question every person in the kiln asks — is: how long? How much longer does the firing have to continue? When does the vessel come out? When does the wine come?

The answer the Potter gives is not a date. It is a principle. The vessel comes out when it is ready to hold what He intends to pour in. Not one day before — because an unfinished vessel breaks under the weight of new wine and both are lost. Not one day after — because the Potter is not cruel and does not keep the vessel in the fire beyond what the vessel requires.

When the vessel is ready, the wine arrives. And when the wine arrives in a prepared vessel, it does not produce a modest, modest output proportional to the modest expectations of a modest season. It produces 82 albums in 8 months from a 46-year-old man who had never touched music production before. It produces 8 books from a man who had never written a full-length book before. It produces a testimony so undeniable that investigators travel to South Carolina looking for a natural explanation and come back empty-handed.

You cannot pour new wine into an old vessel. But you also cannot stop new wine from flowing when the vessel is ready and the Potter decides to pour.

Read this book as evidence that Yahuah finishes what He starts. Read it as documentation that the kiln is not the enemy of the vessel — it is the maker of the vessel. Read it as testimony that the wine is worth the waiting, worth the firing, worth every season that looked like abandonment and was actually preparation.

The vessel is new. The wine is real. The testimony is in your hands.

By design. Not by chance.

— John Alan Legette Keystone, Colorado April 2026

TABLE OF CONTENTS

Front Matter

Introduction

PART ONE: UNDERSTANDING THE BATTLEFIELD

Chapter One: Understanding the Battlefield

Chapter Two: The Circle Walk

CLOSING

Closing Chapter: There Is Still an Elohim in Yahshar'el

- Final Declarations

By Design, Not By Chance

Introduction – The Book You Are Holding Should Not Exist

Opening Epigraph

"The steps of a good man are ordered by Yahuah: and he delighteth in his way. Though he fall, he shall not be utterly cast down: for Yahuah upholdeth him with his hand." — Psalm 37:23-24

"And we know that all things work together for good to them that love Elohim, to them who are the called according to his purpose." — Romans 8:28

Let Me Tell You What Should Have Happened

On the evening of December 10, 2025, someone broke into our home at 7830 South Kingston Avenue, Apartment 3, in Chicago, Illinois. They did not simply enter unlawfully. They kicked the door in — a deliberate act of force designed to accomplish one primary objective: to stop what had begun inside those walls.

What had begun inside those walls was a ministry.

On July 31, 2025 — exactly four months and ten days before the home invasion — my wife and I had begun recording music at that address that would become the foundation of the largest Hebrew Roots music catalog in documented history. In those four months at 7830 South Kingston, we had been building something. Albums were being produced. Teachings were being recorded. The oil of the Ruach HaQodesh had begun to flow after 18 years of creative silence, and what was coming out of that apartment on the South Side of Chicago was unmistakably anointed. It carried the sacred names Yahuah and Yahshua. It carried Torah-based revelation. It carried the weight of decades of preparation being released into sound.

On December 10, 2025, adversaries decided that what was building in that apartment needed to be stopped.

They were wrong. Not because their action failed to displace us — it did displace us. But because displacement, in the economy of Yahuah, is never destruction. It is always distribution.

My King Saul — And What He Was Actually Protecting

I need to tell you something about the nature of the pursuit I have been under, because it contains a theological lesson that goes beyond my personal story and speaks to every believer who has ever been opposed not for what they did wrong but for what Yahuah is about to do right.

I am not going to name the people who have been hunting me. That is not what this section is for. What this section is for is to explain the spiritual logic of why people with resources, influence, and institutional access spend years — in my case, five years of aggressive pursuit and ten years of secret investigation before that — trying to stop someone who has never raised a hand against them and who, by their own admission when I told them directly, had the ability to bring consequences upon them and chose not to.

The answer is not hatred, though hatred may be present. The answer is not simple jealousy, though jealousy may be a component. The answer is promotion.

Saul was not merely a jealous king threatened by a talented shepherd boy. Saul was a king with a succession plan. He intended the throne of Israel to pass to someone of his own choosing. His son Jonathan was the natural heir. His lineage, his legacy, his continued influence over the direction of the nation — all of this was bound up in his ability to determine who came next. And when the Spirit of Yahuah fell on David and the people began to sing *Saul has slain his thousands, and David his ten thousands* — Saul did not hear a compliment being paid to a gifted young man. He heard the sound of his succession plan collapsing. He heard the announcement of a promotion he had not authorized and could not control. And that sound drove him to spend the remaining years of his reign pursuing a man who had done nothing to him, who had served him faithfully, who had played music that quieted the very torment Saul was suffering.

The pursuit was never about what David had done. It was about what Yahuah was about to do.

My situation has followed this same architecture with a precision that I can only describe as scriptural. The people pursuing me are not primarily reacting to anything I have done to harm them. They are reacting to something they have perceived about where I am going. Somewhere in the ten years they spent investigating me secretly, and in the five years they spent pursuing me openly, they arrived at a conclusion about my trajectory — about the promotion that Yahuah has been preparing — and they made a decision that is identical to the decision Saul made: if the promotion happens, it threatens what they have built, what they have planned, and what they intended to pass on to those they have chosen.

They believe my promotion equals their fall.

And here is the most important thing I can say about that belief: they are wrong. Not because my promotion is not real — I believe with everything in me that Yahuah is promoting what He has been preparing in me for decades. But because my promotion and their fall are not the same event. They are not causally connected. They do not happen because of each other. Psalm 75:6-7 says it with a clarity that I have meditated on throughout every mile of this journey: *"For promotion cometh neither from the east, nor from the west, nor from the south. But Elohim is the judge: he putteth down one, and setteth up another."*

Promotion comes from Yahuah. Demotion comes from Yahuah. The two are parallel sovereign acts, not a transaction between two human parties. I have no say in whether Yahuah decides to promote me. That is entirely His decision, made in His counsel before my formation, executed on His timeline without my input. And I have equally no say in whether Yahuah decides to demote them. That too is entirely His decision, made in His counsel, executed on His timeline. The two things are happening in the same season, but they are not happening because of each other. They are both happening because Yahuah is the judge.

I made this clear to my King Saul directly. The way David came out of the cave at En Gedi holding the corner of Saul's robe — not as a threat, but as a declaration of mercy chosen — I told them plainly that they had been placed in my hands. Twice. And I had not taken the opportunity either time, though I could have. I was not seeking their destruction. I was seeking my freedom. All I wanted was to be released from the pursuit and allowed to walk in the assignment Yahuah had given me without being hunted.

Their response to that declaration was the home invasion on December 10, 2025, and the illegal eviction that drove us from Chicago.

I want you to feel the full weight of that. I came to them with the corner of the robe. I said: I am not your enemy. I never was. I do not want to take you down. I want to be free. And they responded by kicking in our door.

That is the moment I understood completely what I was dealing with. Not a misunderstanding that could be resolved with honest conversation. Not a conflict that goodwill could bridge. A King Saul who had passed the point where mercy registers as mercy and now only registers as weakness to be exploited. When Saul saw that David had spared him in the cave, he wept and said *"Thou art more righteous than I"* — but he went right back to pursuing him. The acknowledgment of mercy did not produce repentance. It produced shame, and shame without repentance produces escalation.

So they escalated.

And the escalation sent us to O'Hare Airport on December 11, 2025. And O'Hare sent us to Phoenix. And Phoenix sent us to Crescent City. And Crescent City sent us up through ten states and ten thousand to twenty thousand miles and sixteen weeks to Keystone, Colorado at 9,280 feet above sea level, where 82 albums and this book and 589 teachings and the largest Hebrew Roots music catalog in documented history were waiting to be unlocked by the compressive force of everything they sent against us.

They funded the testimony they were trying to prevent.

They supplied the pressure that activated the arch they were trying to collapse. They spent five years of aggressive pursuit accomplishing the opposite of what they intended — because Yahuah is the architect, and He does not allow compressive force to be applied to His structures without incorporating it into the design.

I have never wanted their destruction. I want to say that one more time so it is permanently on the record. Not in this book, not in any legal proceeding, not in any conversation private or public, have I desired the destruction of the people who have been pursuing me. What I desired was the freedom to walk in my assignment. Yahuah granted that freedom — not by removing the pursuit, but by turning the pressure of the pursuit into the productive force that drove 52 albums out of me in the first three months of the tour alone.

The pursuit paid for the testimony. Let Yahuah be the judge of everything else. He put Saul on the throne. He took Saul off the throne. He put David on the throne. None of those three decisions required David's participation. None of them required David's vengeance. None of them required anything from David except covenant faithfulness and the refusal to raise his hand against what Yahuah had not yet judged.

I am still making that same choice.

To every believer who is reading this book and recognizing their own King Saul in these pages — someone who is pursuing you not because of what you have done but because of where Yahuah is taking you, someone who has mistaken your coming promotion for their inevitable fall, someone who has responded to your mercy with escalation — I need you to hear this with everything I have:

Do not take the corner of the robe.

Not because they do not deserve consequences. Not because justice is not coming. But because the judge of all the earth will do right, and He does not need your hand on the sword to accomplish it. Your King Saul's demotion is not your assignment. Your promotion is your assignment. Keep your eyes on the assignment. Let Yahuah handle the verdict.

"For promotion cometh neither from the east, nor from the west, nor from the south. But Elohim is the judge: he putteth down one, and setteth up another." — Psalm 75:6-7

"Yahuah shall fight for you, and ye shall hold your peace." — Exodus 14:14

The peace I held while being hunted for five years produced 82 albums, 589 teachings, 8 books, and the testimony you are now reading.

Hold your peace. Let Yahuah fight. The promotion is coming. And it is coming by design — not by chance.

What Happened the Next Morning

On December 11, 2025 — the morning after our home was invaded and we were forced out — my wife and I did not collapse. We did not retreat into the system that had held us for years. We did not return to the people who had driven us out and accept the terms they were offering.

We went to O'Hare International Airport.

We caught a flight.

And the unplanned evangelical tour of the American West began.

I need you to sit with the timing of that for a moment, because the theology of this entire book lives in the gap between December 10th and December 11th. One day. Twelve hours, perhaps, between the moment our home was violated and the moment we were in the air. We did not plan the tour. We did not have an itinerary. We did not have a team, a budget, a booking agent, or a strategy. We had a covenant relationship with Yahuah, a wife who trusted the same covenant, whatever was in our hands when we walked out the door, and the direction of the Ruach.

That was enough. That has always been enough.

The Hub and the Journey

Phoenix Sky Harbor Airport became our transportation hub from that day forward. We did not plan that either. It simply became the place to which we returned between assignments — the staging area from which the Ruach deployed us to the next location, the next elevation, the next season of the assignment. Over the course of the next sixteen weeks, we rented cars from Phoenix and drove them across the American West. We returned to Phoenix to exchange one car for another and then set out again in the direction the Ruach indicated. We drove approximately ten thousand to twenty thousand miles. We passed through ten states: Arizona, Nevada, New Mexico, Colorado, Wyoming, Utah, Idaho, Montana, California, and Oregon.

Phoenix sits at approximately 1,086 feet above sea level. Chicago, where the journey began, sits at approximately 596 feet above sea level. And what I did not know when we boarded that flight from O'Hare on December 11th — what I could not have known, because no human being designed this itinerary — was that every significant location to which the Ruach would lead us from that day forward would be higher than the place we had just left. The journey that began at 596 feet in Chicago was going to ascend, location by location, elevation by elevation, until it reached the apex of an arch that Yahuah had been constructing since before my formation.

But I am getting ahead of myself. Let me tell you the sequence as it actually happened.

The First Album on the Tour: Crescent City, California

The flight from O'Hare did not take us directly west. The Ruach took us through San Diego first — we spent a night in the San Diego Airport, which is its own kind of wilderness experience — and then we flew to San Francisco. From San Francisco we rented a car and drove north along the California coast to Crescent City, California.

Crescent City sits at approximately 40 to 50 feet above sea level. It is a coastal town at the edge of the Pacific Ocean, surrounded by ancient redwood forests, perched at the northwestern corner of California where the land meets water and the sky feels wider than anywhere I had stood before. It is, by elevation, the lowest point of the entire western journey. Sea level. The base of everything.

And it is where we wrote and produced the first album of the unplanned evangelical tour.

I did not understand the significance of that in the moment. I understand it now. Every arch begins at its lowest point and curves upward toward the apex. Every progressive altitude sequence begins at the ground. Crescent City — at sea level, at the edge of the continent, in the first days after being driven from our home — was the ground course of the arch. The first stone placed on the western journey. The beginning of the upward curve.

We drove back to San Francisco after completing that album, exchanged the car, and drove east to Yosemite Valley, which sits at approximately 4,000 feet above sea level. The valley floor of Yosemite is surrounded by granite walls that rise thousands of feet in every direction. It is a place of geological enormity — a space that communicates, without a single word, the smallness of the human frame and the magnitude of the One who shaped the stone. We were there briefly, but the elevation had already begun to climb.

From Yosemite we made our way back to Phoenix —
back to the hub, back to the staging area — and the
Ruach prepared the next deployment.

The Progressive Altitude Pattern

What happened next, over the following weeks and
months, was not something I orchestrated. I present the
sequence here not as a travel itinerary but as evidence
— documented, GPS-verified, chronologically
established evidence — that the path we walked was
designed by Someone who knew where it was going
before we took the first step.

From Phoenix at 1,086 feet, we were deployed to
Hurricane, Utah, sitting at approximately 3,250 feet
above sea level. Hurricane is a modest town in the high
desert of southwestern Utah, and it is where the creative
silence of 18 years first broke open in full force on the
road. The oil did not trickle. It flowed. Albums began to
be produced at a rate that I cannot attribute to any
natural capacity. I am a trained musician with decades
of preparation behind me, but what came out of me in
Hurricane was not the product of training alone. It was
the product of stored anointing meeting its appointed
moment of release. Hurricane at 3,250 feet is where
Yahuah confirmed that the tour was not just a
displacement event. It was a creative commission.

From Hurricane we moved through Moab, Utah, at
approximately 4,025 to 6,200 feet — a canyon country
of red rock and desert sky where the silence is so

complete that it becomes its own form of communication. The elevation was rising. The output was accelerating.

From Moab we traveled to Garden City, Utah, situated on the shores of Bear Lake at approximately 5,900 feet — a place of quiet so particular that revelation arrived there with an immediacy I had not experienced before. High places thin the noise. They create conditions for the kind of clarity that lower elevations make difficult.

We stayed in Victor, Idaho, at approximately 6,200 feet — thirty minutes from Jackson Hole, Wyoming, and the Grand Teton mountain range. I want to say something about the Grand Teton directly, because it is impossible to stand near those mountains and not feel what they communicate. The Grand Teton rises to 13,770 to 13,775 feet above sea level. The valley floor of Jackson Hole sits at approximately 6,320 to 6,400 feet. The mountains rise more than 7,000 vertical feet from the valley base with no foothills between them — they simply erupt from the earth without preamble, the most dramatic vertical rise in the Rocky Mountains. They are the youngest mountains in the range, formed by a massive fault block uplift, and they look exactly like what they are: something driven upward by an irresistible force from below.

I filed that image away. I did not fully understand it yet.

From Victor we moved through Estes Park, Colorado, at approximately 7,522 feet — just east of Rocky Mountain National Park, whose peaks range from 7,860 feet to over 14,000 feet. Estes Park was where the elevation pattern became undeniable to me. I was not going to lower ground. Every location was higher than the last. The arch was curving upward in a sequence that no travel agent had planned and no human strategy had arranged.

And then we came to Florence, Colorado.

Florence: The Costliest Voussoir

Florence, Colorado sits at approximately 5,190 feet above sea level. Florence was not about its absolute altitude in the sequence. Florence was about harvest — and about the cost of harvest when the enemy understands what is being produced.

Florence was the location where 21 albums were produced in 24 days inside The Rosemont, Florence Centennial Historic Structure 59, at 431 East 2nd Street — a building constructed in 1887 that my wife and I entered on February 28, 2026, as the first Black couple in its 139-year history. What happened in Florence is documented in full in Chapter Ten of this book. What I will say here is this: Florence was the most productive and the most opposed location of the entire journey simultaneously. The greatest single-location creative outpouring of the entire catalog occurred inside a building that was simultaneously the site of the most concentrated and legally documentable opposition we had faced since leaving Chicago.

The two facts are inseparable. They belong together. They explain each other.

We stayed. We completed the assignment. We departed on March 28, 2026, as scheduled, having fulfilled every term of our agreement, having broken no law, having harmed no one, having produced 21 albums inside walls that had never heard the sacred names Yahuah and Yahshua proclaimed in covenant worship. We walked out carrying a testimony that no subsequent act of opposition can recall or erase.

Keystone: The Apex

From Florence, Yahuah sent us to Keystone, Colorado.

Keystone sits at a base elevation of approximately 9,280 feet above sea level, with surrounding peaks continuing to rise beyond that. It is the highest point in the documented journey. It is also, architecturally, the most important point — the apex of an arch that was being constructed from the moment we left Chicago at 596 feet. The progressive elevation sequence, from the South Side of Chicago to the summit of Keystone, is not a travel pattern. It is a structural design. And the name itself — Keystone — is the architectural term for the wedge-shaped stone placed last at the summit of a masonry arch, the stone that locks every other stone into its permanent load-bearing position.

I am a trained architect. When the Ruach sent us to a city called Keystone, I did not need to look up what the name meant. I already knew. And I understood immediately that the arch Yahuah had been building through every location of this journey — from sea level in Crescent City to the alpine summit of Keystone — had just received its apex stone.

The centering — the temporary scaffolding of human strategy, human resources, and human explanation — could now be removed. The structure was standing on its own.

The Complete Elevation Record

For the reader who processes evidence visually, here is the documented elevation sequence of the unplanned evangelical tour of 2025 and 2026, from the point of origin to the apex:

Location	Elevation	Significance
Chicago, IL (7830 S. Kingston)	~596 ft	Ministry origin; point of displacement
San Diego, CA (overnight)	~62 ft	Transit point; wilderness night
Crescent City, CA	~40–50 ft	First album of the tour
Yosemite Valley, CA	~4,000 ft	Valley floor; ascending begins
Phoenix, AZ (hub)	~1,086 ft	Transportation base; repeated returns

Location	Elevation	Significance
Hurricane, UT	~3,250 ft	Creative silence breaks open
Moab, UT	~4,025–6,200 ft	Elevation principle confirmed
Garden City, UT	~5,900+ ft	Quiet revelation; Bear Lake
Victor, ID	~6,200 ft	Covenant endurance; near Grand Teton
Florence, CO	~5,190 ft	Harvest season; 21 albums in 24 days
Estes Park, CO	~7,522 ft	Pattern confirmed intentional
Keystone, CO	~9,280 ft	Apex stone; all streams locked

This table was not constructed in advance. It was assembled by looking back at where the Ruach had led and recognizing that no random itinerary produces a sequence this deliberately ascending. Every location was in the book Psalm 139:16 describes — written before a single day of the journey was lived. Every elevation was calculated by the architect before the first stone was placed.

What This Book Is

This book is the documented testimony of an unplanned evangelical tour that began with a home invasion in Chicago on December 10, 2025, and became the largest Hebrew Roots music catalog in documented history across sixteen weeks, ten states, and ten thousand to twenty thousand miles of driving through the American West.

It is the testimony of an 18-year creative drought that ended not when circumstances became comfortable — they never did — but when the appointed moment of release arrived and the stored oil of the Ruach broke open.

It is the testimony of an elevation pattern that no human being designed, leading from the lowest ground at the edge of the Pacific Ocean to the highest peaks of the Colorado Rockies, with creative output increasing at every elevation and adversarial opposition intensifying at the most significant location — because the enemy always concentrates his forces at the points of greatest anointing.

It is the testimony of a covenant relationship with Yahuah that held through homelessness, creative drought, displacement, opposition, surveillance, property damage, police suppression, communication interference, and sustained pursuit across multiple state lines by people who believed my promotion was connected to their fall.

It is the testimony of 82 albums, 1,180 tracks, 589 YouTube teachings, and 8 books — including this one

— produced in eight months with no studio, no budget, no team, no label, and no fixed address. All of it produced while homeless. All of it produced while being hunted. All of it produced because the Ruach of Yahuah does not require favorable circumstances in order to move. He requires a surrendered vessel. That is all. He requires a vessel that will stay inside the building when the adversaries are circling outside, keep the sacred names on its lips, and let the oil flow.

This book is the answer to the question the adversaries have been asking for years: how is he so favored? How does a man with no resources, no team, no infrastructure, no stable address, and sustained pursuit against him produce at a rate that exceeds most full ministry careers in the span of months?

The answer is in the title. It is not by chance. It was never by chance. It was by design — the design of an architect whose blueprints were completed before the author of this book drew his first breath, whose construction timeline was not disrupted by a home invasion on December 10, 2025, and whose completed structure now stands at 9,280 feet above sea level, locked into permanent position by the apex stone of a sequence that began at the edge of the Pacific Ocean and ascended without reversal to the summit of the Colorado Rockies.

They funded the testimony they were trying to prevent.

And the testimony is now in your hands.

A Note on Sacred Names

Throughout this book, I use the sacred Hebrew names Yahuah and Yahshua rather than the titles God, Lord, and Jesus. This is not an act of religious superiority or tribal exclusivity. It is an act of covenant fidelity. Yahuah is the personal, covenantal name of the Creator of all things, revealed to Moshe at the burning bush and declared as His memorial name to all generations. Yahshua is the Hebrew name of the Messiah, meaning Yahuah is salvation. These names appear more than 6,800 times in the original Hebrew scriptures. I use them because they are His names, and the testimony recorded in these pages belongs to the One whose name is on it.

If you are not familiar with these names, I invite you to receive the testimony without letting the names become a barrier. The Elohim this book testifies about is the same One who parted the Red Sea, who fed five thousand with five loaves, who raised the dead and opened blind eyes, and who turned a home invasion in Chicago into a sixteen-week, ten-state, mountain-climbing ministry tour that produced 82 albums and this book. Whatever name you have known Him by, He is real, He is faithful, and He fights for His children.

How to Read This Book

This book is both testimony and teaching — a combination of first-person narrative and theological instruction that moves between the personal and the principled throughout every chapter. The personal sections tell you what happened. The teaching sections tell you what it means and how it applies to your own life and assignment.

You do not need to be in the same tradition to receive this testimony. You need only to be honest about the season you are in. If you are in a drought, this book was written for you. If you are under sustained opposition, this book was written for you. If you have been displaced and do not yet understand that displacement and distribution are the same event in the economy of Yahuah, this book was written for you. If you are running from your own King Saul and you need someone to tell you that holding your peace while being hunted is not weakness but covenant confidence, this book was written for you. If you need documented, timestamped, GPS-verified evidence that the covenant protection of Yahuah is real and active and structurally superior to every opposing force, this book is that evidence.

Read it. Receive it. Let the testimony do what testimonies are designed to do — build faith for your own next step, your own next elevation, your own approaching apex.

The arch is being built. Every stone is in the drawings. The keystone is coming.

By design. Not by chance.

Chapter One begins on the following page.

---

*The Introduction is complete. Say **"Write the Foreword"** when you are ready, and we will complete the full manuscript with the declaration that frames everything before the reader enters the Introduction.*

CHAPTER ONE

Understanding the Battlefield

What Is Color Magic and Why Do People Use It

"My people are destroyed for lack of knowledge."

— Hoshea 4:6

In My Own Words — John Alan Legette

I want to begin this chapter with something important.

I am not a fearful man.

I say that not as a boast but as a necessary context for everything you are about to read. When I began researching the subject of color magic and the broader landscape of occult spiritual practice being directed against me, I did not approach that research from a place of anxiety, paranoia, or spiritual instability. I approached it the same way a soldier approaches a briefing on enemy tactics — with calm attention, strategic interest, and the settled confidence of someone who already knows the outcome of the war even while the individual battles are still being fought. The covenant I stand in is unambiguous on this point. Numbers 23:23 declares it plainly — there is no enchantment against Jacob, nor divination against Israel. Isaiah 54:17 seals it — no weapon formed against me shall prosper, and every tongue that rises against me in judgment I shall condemn. This is the heritage of the servants of Yahuah.

I stand in that heritage. And from that position of covenant security, I began to understand the battlefield.

What I discovered through careful research and through the direct spiritual discernment that Yahuah had been sharpening in me through years of sustained opposition was not surprising in its existence but was illuminating in its specificity. People have been using color, direction, physical objects, and coordinated spiritual intention to work against other people for thousands of years. The practices are documented across cultures, across centuries, and across continents. They are real in the sense that people genuinely practice them with genuine intent. And understanding how they work — what each element means, what each color is intended to accomplish, what each physical action is designed to initiate — is not a journey into darkness. It is the application of Hoshea 4:6 in reverse. My people are destroyed for lack of knowledge. Knowledge, applied from a position of covenant authority, does not destroy. It protects.

Let me share with you what I learned. And then let me show you what the covenant says about all of it.

What I Was Dealing With

Before I explain the mechanics of color magic and related practices, let me give you enough context to understand why this knowledge became necessary and personal for me rather than merely academic.

I am in a conflict — and I use that word deliberately and without exaggeration — with people who operate in the realm of occult spiritual practice and who have recruited networks across multiple states and beyond with one specific objective. That objective is my suppression, my control, and ultimately my destruction. The reason for this conflict is straightforward. I inadvertently exposed these people publicly. What was hidden was brought into the light. And people whose power depends entirely on secrecy and the absence of accountability do not respond to exposure with gracious acknowledgment. They respond with total war.

The opening salvo of that war — at least the opening salvo that I was personally present to witness — happened in a hotel lobby. A man walked a deliberate circle around my wife and me. That single act was the visible surface of something much more layered and much more specifically executed than a casual hotel guest looking for his luggage. By the time that night was over there was a muddy footprint on the back patio of our ground floor room, a stick positioned in a chair pointing directly toward the window behind which we slept, and a specific arrangement of vehicles outside our room in a color pattern of white, gray, blue, and black that I will explain in full detail in the next chapter.

I will tell you the full account of that night in Chapter Two. But before I can tell that story with the full weight it deserves, I need to give you the knowledge that makes the story comprehensible. Because what happened in that hotel was not random. It was a vocabulary — a specific, intentional, layered vocabulary drawn from traditions of magical practice that have been in continuous use for centuries. And you cannot read a vocabulary you have never been taught.

So let me teach it to you. Not so that you can use it. But so that you can recognize it, name it, refuse it, and stand against it from the position of covenant authority that makes every working directed at a child of the covenant ultimately powerless.

TEACHING: Understanding Color Magic — What It Is and How It Works

A Teaching for Every Believer Who Needs to Know the Enemy's Vocabulary

Color magic is one of the oldest and most widely practiced forms of intentional spiritual working across many traditions — including Wicca, Paganism, folk magic, Hoodoo, various indigenous practices, and numerous esoteric systems that have existed in continuous operation from ancient Egypt and Greece through to the present day. To understand it you do not need to enter into it. You only need to understand its logic, its vocabulary, and its mechanics — the same way a physician understands the biology of a pathogen without becoming infected by it.

The Foundation: What Color Magic Actually Is

At its foundation, color magic operates on a single governing principle — that each color carries a specific energetic frequency or vibrational quality that can be deliberately invoked, focused, and directed toward a specific purpose or a specific person. This is not entirely without parallel in the natural world. Light itself behaves scientifically in exactly the way the practitioners describe metaphysically — different colors literally exist on different wavelengths, and the documented field of chromotherapy, which uses colored light therapeutically to address emotional and physical conditions, is the clinical descendant of what ancient cultures understood intuitively about the relationship between color and human experience.

In practical application, color magic is worked through specific physical anchors — candles of specific colors burned with specific intentions, clothing worn deliberately to project or absorb specific energies, altar cloths, ribbons, inks, papers, crystals, herbs, and visualization exercises in which specific colors are mentally projected toward or around a target. The color chosen becomes both a symbolic and an energetic anchor for the practitioner's intention. And this is the critical point that separates color magic from mere decoration or aesthetic preference — color magic is not passive. It requires focused, deliberate, sustained intention. Most practitioners across all traditions would agree that the intention behind the color is the true engine of the working. The color is the vehicle. The will is the fuel.

This is also why the covenant declaration of Numbers 23:23 is so architecturally precise as a counter to this practice. The working requires the will of the practitioner to penetrate the spiritual atmosphere around the target. But when the target is covered by the covenant of Yahuah, the spiritual atmosphere around them is not accessible to the will of an outside practitioner. The working hits a wall it cannot penetrate. The fuel burns but the vehicle goes nowhere. We will return to this principle at the end of this chapter when we discuss the covenant response to everything the enemy deploys.

Why Someone Would Direct Color Magic Against Another Person

Most color magic — in the way its practitioners understand and describe it — is used for personal purposes. Healing, protection, manifestation, emotional balance, and the attraction of desired outcomes are the most commonly cited applications. In this sense color magic functions as a kind of spiritual technology that practitioners use to influence their own lives and circumstances.

But color magic can also be weaponized. Directed outward toward a specific person with specific hostile intent, the same colors that are used for healing and protection become instruments of suppression, confusion, domination, and harm. A practitioner might direct color magic against another person for several reasons — jealousy, the desire for control, revenge, obsession, or the need for spiritual dominance over someone who represents a threat to their power or their secrets.

The ethics of this practice vary widely by tradition. Many practitioners draw a firm line between defensive and offensive use and operate according to versions of the principle that what is sent returns to the sender multiplied — a principle that is, interestingly, entirely consistent with the scriptural teaching of Psalm 7:15-16, which describes the person who digs a pit for another falling into it themselves. But the ethical restraints of any tradition only govern practitioners who choose to be governed by them. The people who direct occult practice against others with malicious intent are, by definition, operating outside of every ethical restraint their own tradition might offer.

Understanding that someone would target another person this way requires understanding what drives the obsession behind it. We will cover that psychology in full in Chapter Three. For now, understand simply this — when someone has the knowledge, the tools, the will, and the motivation to direct spiritual working against another person, color becomes one of their primary instruments because it is both versatile and difficult for an untrained observer to detect or identify. A person who walks into a room where a specific color working has been laid against them will experience its effects without necessarily knowing what they are experiencing or why. That invisibility is part of what makes color-based working attractive to those who practice offensive spiritual targeting.

The Five Colors and Their Offensive Applications

What follows is a detailed breakdown of the five specific colors that were being used against me — black, white, blue, red, and gray — including both their general properties in magical tradition and their specific applications when directed against another person with hostile intent. This knowledge is not presented to frighten you. It is presented to equip you with the vocabulary to recognize what you may be seeing if you encounter these patterns in your own experience.

Black — The Color of Banishment, Suppression, and Psychic Attack

Black is simultaneously the most powerful and the most misunderstood color in magical practice. In its protective and defensive application, black is used to absorb and deflect negative energy, banish unwanted influences, and create a strong barrier of spiritual protection around the practitioner. A person using black defensively is essentially wrapping themselves in a spiritual absorber — pulling in whatever is directed at them and neutralizing it before it can land.

But black in its offensive application — directed toward another person with hostile intent — takes on a fundamentally different character. Black candle workings directed toward a specific individual are associated with banishment spells, which are rituals designed to forcefully remove a person from a space, a relationship, a sphere of influence, or a life entirely. More extreme applications involve binding spells, in which black is used to restrict, freeze, or suppress a person's actions, their authority, their gifts, or their ability to function in their calling. Hex workings using black are intended to bring misfortune, confusion, spiritual heaviness, and a sense of darkness or being oppressed into the target's life and atmosphere.

A well-documented technique involves writing a person's name on black cloth or paper and burning it with a black candle while focusing the intention on driving that person away or neutralizing their power. The symbolic logic is straightforward — the burning removes, the black absorbs, and the combined working says to the universe of the practitioner's belief system — I am extinguishing this person's light, removing their presence, and suppressing their influence.

What black directed against you essentially declares is this — I am removing you. I am suppressing you. I am darkening your path.

For a believer standing in covenant, the response to that declaration is Psalm 18:28 — *For You will light my lamp. Yahuah my Elohim will enlighten my darkness.* No working can extinguish what Yahuah has lit. No binding can suppress what He has commissioned. And no banishment can remove from the path He has established the vessel He has placed upon it.

White — The Color of Exposure, Truth-Stripping, and Spiritual Surveillance

White carries an almost universally positive reputation in popular spiritual culture — it is associated with purity, healing, consecration, blessings, and divine connection, and it is often considered the most versatile color in magical practice because of its association with undirected pure energy. In its benevolent application white is genuinely powerful for exactly these purposes.

But white in its offensive application is used in a way that most people do not anticipate. White directed against another person with hostile intent becomes a tool for exposure — for truth-revealing workings designed to strip away every covering, every protection of privacy, every hidden dimension of a person's life and force it into visibility. Think of white in this context not as light that illuminates in a healing sense but as a spiritual searchlight aimed directly at whatever a practitioner wants to uncover about their target. The intent is to leave nothing hidden — to expose weaknesses, secrets, vulnerabilities, and anything that could be used as leverage or ammunition against the target.

When combined with the domination intention — the desire to control a person by possessing information about them that they have not chosen to share — white becomes a surveillance tool in the spiritual realm. It is the magical equivalent of a wire tap. The practitioner is not trying to harm the target directly with white. They are trying to see everything about the target so that what they find can be used to harm, control, or leverage them through other means.

This is particularly significant in the context of the conflict I have been navigating. The people pursuing me have been explicitly trying to find something — any information, any weakness, any vulnerability, any dirt or leverage — that they could use to control me or compromise my credibility. The use of white in this offensive configuration is entirely consistent with that objective. They are not just trying to destroy me directly. They are trying to find the thing that will give them power over me. White, in this application, is their spiritual search warrant.

The covenant response is Job 12:22 — *He reveals the deep things of darkness and brings utter darkness into the light.* What Yahuah chooses to keep covered is covered. What He chooses to reveal, He reveals in His own time and for His own purposes. No practitioner's white working can override the covering of the Most High over what He has chosen to protect.

Blue — The Color of Emotional Manipulation, Mental Influence, and Vulnerability Exploitation

Blue in its gentle and benevolent application is associated with peace, healing, emotional balance, communication, and the development of discernment. Light blue connects to the throat — the center of honest communication and trust — while darker blue connects to intuition and emotional depth. In worship contexts blue carries the associations of the heavenly realm, the vastness of the sky, and the depth of Yahuah's presence.

But blue directed against another person with manipulative intent becomes something quite different. It becomes a tool for emotional and mental influence — for workings designed to make a target more open, more emotionally vulnerable, more communicative about things they would otherwise keep private, and more susceptible to trusting the wrong people at the wrong moments. When someone directs blue energy toward another person without their knowledge or consent, they are essentially attempting to lower the emotional and mental defenses of that person — to dissolve the healthy boundaries that would otherwise prevent them from being manipulated, deceived, or exploited.

Dark blue specifically, in occult tradition, is associated with the exploitation of emotional vulnerability — increasing feelings of depression, emotional dependence, and confusion in the target, and clouding their spiritual discernment so that they cannot perceive clearly what is being done to them or who is doing it. A person who has been the target of a sustained blue working may experience inexplicable emotional openness, a sudden tendency to trust the wrong people, confusion in their discernment, or a general sense of emotional exposure and vulnerability that has no obvious natural explanation.

The covenant response is Philippians 4:7 — *And the peace of Yahuah, which surpasses all understanding, will guard your hearts and your minds in Yahshua HaMashaich.* The guard that the peace of Yahuah places around the heart and mind of a covenant believer is not accessible to the manipulative blue working of an outside practitioner. The emotional and mental territory that blue is attempting to access is territory that has already been occupied and protected by the Ruach of Yahuah.

Red — The Color of Domination, Aggression, and the Inflaming of Conflict

Red is perhaps the most dynamically powerful color in magical tradition — tied to passion, love, lust, courage, war, strength, the life force, and the most primal dimensions of human experience. It governs the most foundational energetic center — the root, the place of survival, safety, and the basic human drives. In its positive application red is associated with courage, vitality, and the kind of passionate commitment that drives significant achievement.

But red in its offensive application is one of the most aggressive colors available to a practitioner working against a target. Domination spells using red are designed to overpower another person's will — to make them subservient, compliant, or unable to resist the demands of the practitioner. This is not metaphorical. Domination working is specifically aimed at breaking a person's spiritual and psychological autonomy — at making them a controlled instrument of someone else's agenda rather than a free vessel operating under their own covenant authority.

Red is also used in lust workings — intended to provoke intense desire or obsession in a target, binding their emotional and physical attention to the practitioner in ways that compromise their judgment and their freedom. And in conflict magic, red is invoked to fuel aggression — to stoke anger in the target or in the target's relationships, to bring war and chaos into their life, to inflame whatever tensions already exist and push them toward destructive expression. Red energy directed at a person essentially amplifies whatever is already within them — passion becomes obsession, courage becomes recklessness, and strength becomes uncontrolled aggression that damages the relationships and the credibility of the target.

What makes red particularly dangerous in the context of someone whose enemies want to suppress and control them is this — a person consumed by inflamed, uncontrolled passion, anger, or conflict is a person who is distracted from their assignment, compromised in their credibility, and ultimately easier to manipulate and destroy. Red is not just about direct harm. It is about creating internal chaos in the target that becomes its own weapon against them.

The covenant response is Proverbs 25:28 — *A man without self-control is like a city broken into and left without walls.* But the covenant also provides the walls. A person whose spirit is governed by the Ruach of Yahuah and whose peace rests on the foundation of the tested stone cannot be inflamed by a red working because the Ruach produces self-control as one of its consistent fruits. What the working is trying to ignite has already been brought under the governance of the One who cannot be manipulated by the intentions of outside practitioners.

Gray — The Color of Confusion, Neutralization, and Psychic Fog

Gray occupies a unique position in magical tradition that is often underestimated precisely because of its subtlety. It sits in the space between black and white — neither fully dark nor fully light — and it is associated with what practitioners call gray magic, a category of working that is neither clearly benevolent nor clearly harmful but operates in the ambiguous middle territory. Gray is the color of neutrality, ambiguity, and the erasure of strong energies in either direction.

When directed against another person, gray is most commonly used in confusion workings — its purpose being to cloud the target's thinking, dull their instincts, neutralize their spiritual power, and create what practitioners describe as a psychic fog around the target so that they cannot see clearly, make sound decisions, or take the kind of decisive action that their assignment requires. Gray is the enemy of clarity, of sharp discernment, and of the kind of confident forward momentum that a person operating in their calling needs to maintain.

Gray is also used in workings designed to make a person socially invisible — to diminish their presence in the eyes of others, to cause them to be overlooked, dismissed, or forgotten by people who might otherwise support, amplify, or partner with their work. In a ministry context, gray directed against a teacher or a minister is a working aimed at reducing their influence and their reach — making their voice quieter, their message less penetrating, and their presence less memorable to those who encounter it.

When combined with black, gray amplifies banishment and suppression. When combined with white, it softens an aggressive working without eliminating it. And when used as a standalone working sustained over time, gray creates a cumulative effect of mental and spiritual heaviness that the target may experience as a general inability to get traction, a persistent sense of confusion about direction, or an inexplicable reduction in the effectiveness and the reach of what they are doing.

The covenant response is Psalm 32:8 — *I will instruct you and teach you in the way you should go. I will counsel you with My eye upon you.* When Yahuah's eye is on you — when His instruction is flowing and His counsel is active — no psychic fog can obscure the path He has illuminated. The gray working requires the absence of divine direction to create confusion in the target. But a vessel who is in active covenant relationship with the Source of all wisdom and all clarity is a vessel that cannot be kept confused for long, because the clarity keeps coming from a Source the working cannot reach.

The Combined Working — What Layered Color Magic Looks Like

What makes color magic particularly complex and particularly significant when someone is using it against another person is that practitioners rarely work with a single color in isolation. Someone building a comprehensive working against a specific target will layer multiple colors simultaneously or sequentially — each one addressing a different dimension of the target's life and a different aspect of what the practitioner wants to accomplish.

The combination being directed against me — white, gray, blue, black, and red — represents a remarkably comprehensive layered working when you understand what each color is designed to do. White to expose and strip away my spiritual covering and privacy. Gray to create confusion and cloud my discernment. Blue to make me emotionally vulnerable and open to manipulation. Black to suppress, bind, and drive me from my path. And red to inflame conflict in my relationships and stoke the kind of internal and external chaos that would make me easier to destroy.

Together these five colors address virtually every dimension of a person's life — their spiritual covering, their mental clarity, their emotional stability, their forward momentum, and their relational health. This is not a casual or accidental collection. This is a comprehensive strategic working designed by people who understand the vocabulary they are using and have applied it with deliberate intent against a specific target.

What they did not account for is the covenant. They chose the most comprehensive array of colors available to them and directed it at a man covered by the most comprehensive spiritual protection available in the universe. And the result has been documented in the pages of this book with mathematical precision.

The working produced eighty two albums. The working produced five hundred and eighty nine teachings. The working produced the largest Hebrew Roots catalog in history. The working funded a national evangelical tour and placed the sacred names in ears across this country and around the world.

Not because the working was ineffective by its own standards.

Because the covenant it ran into was older, stronger, and infinitely more authoritative than the intentions of the people who deployed it.

What the Covenant Says About All of It

This is the section of this chapter that matters most. Everything that preceded it was intelligence gathering — the enemy's vocabulary, the enemy's tools, the enemy's methodology. This section is the covenant response. And the covenant response does not require pages to make its point, because the point has already been made in a single verse, spoken over the people of Yahuah by a prophet who was brought specifically to curse them and could not do it.

There is no enchantment against Jacob, nor divination against Israel.

Numbers 23:23.

Read it again.

Not — there is limited enchantment against Jacob. Not — enchantment against Jacob is difficult but possible under the right conditions. Not — Jacob has some protection against enchantment but sustained and well-resourced working can eventually break through. There is no enchantment against Jacob. None. The Hebrew word used here is nachash — divination, enchantment, the reading and manipulation of omens. And the declaration over the covenant people is categorical. It does not work. Full stop.

This is not a verse written from a position of ignorance about the existence or the practice of enchantment and divination. The man speaking these words — Balaam — was one of the most accomplished practitioners of exactly these arts in the ancient world. He was hired specifically because of his demonstrated ability to curse effectively. And after standing on the mountain four separate times with the explicit assignment of cursing Israel, he declared under the compulsion of the Ruach of Yahuah what his own professional assessment had concluded — that there is no enchantment against this people because Yahuah their Elohim is with them.

The working does not fail against covenant people because covenant people are inherently powerful. It fails because of Who is with them. The protection is not in the person. The protection is in the Presence.

And Hoshea 4:6 — *my people are destroyed for lack of knowledge* — gives us the one condition under which the covenant protection can be compromised. Not by the power of the practitioner. Not by the sophistication of the working. Not by the resources or the coordination of the people deploying it. By the ignorance of the person it is deployed against. A covenant person who does not know who they are, what they carry, and what is being done to them is vulnerable not because their covering is insufficient but because they are not standing in it consciously and deliberately.

This is why this chapter exists. This is why you needed to read what you just read. Not because knowledge of color magic gives you power over it. But because knowledge of what is being done to you enables you to stand in the covenant that makes it powerless, consciously and specifically and with full spiritual authority, rather than simply hoping that the covering is working while remaining unaware of what is being thrown at it.

Knowing the enemy's vocabulary does not make you afraid of the enemy. It makes you a more effective occupant of the covenant position you already hold.

Practical Covenant Response — What to Do If You Recognize These Patterns

If you are reading this chapter and recognizing patterns in your own experience — specific color arrangements appearing in your environment with deliberate regularity, specific physical objects placed in or around your living space, specific behavioral patterns from people in your life that mirror what has been described in the circle walking tradition we will discuss in Chapter Two — here is the covenant response that is both scripturally grounded and practically effective.

The first response is declaration. Speak Numbers 23:23 and Isaiah 54:17 aloud over yourself, your wife or husband, your children, your home, and your assignment. Do not speak them as wishes. Speak them as covenant facts — because that is what they are. The covenant is not contingent on your feelings about it. It is contingent on the faithfulness of the One who made it. Declare it as the legal reality it is.

The second response is cleansing. Salt applied to doorways and thresholds and then swept away from the building is one of the most consistent cleansing practices across traditions — and it is entirely consistent with the biblical use of salt as a symbol of covenant, preservation, and the absence of corruption. A cleansing bath using sea salt and hyssop, accompanied by prayer and declaration, is a scriptural practice rooted in Psalm 51:7 — *Purge me with hyssop and I shall be clean.* These are not superstitious rituals. They are covenant acts performed with covenant authority by covenant people.

The third response is the removal and disposal of any physical objects that have been deliberately placed in your space. Do not handle them with bare hands if possible. Do not bring them inside your living space. Remove them, dispose of them away from your property — burning or flowing water being the most commonly recommended methods across traditions — and cleanse the area where they were found.

The fourth and most foundational response is worship. Specifically worship in the sacred names. The name Yahuah carries the covenant presence of the One whose authority makes every working directed at His children ultimately powerless. When you worship in that name, you are not merely singing. You are activating the covenant atmosphere around you in the most direct and most powerful way available to a human vessel. You are releasing the breath of Yahuah — the Ruach — into the spiritual atmosphere of your space and your assignment. And nothing that operates in darkness can maintain its position in that atmosphere.

This is, not incidentally, why the music Yahuah has been releasing through me in this season carries the specific authority it carries. Fourteen hundred tracks of worship in the sacred names are not just a music catalog. They are a sustained, global, continuously playing covenant declaration that is doing active spiritual work in the atmospheres of everyone who hears it, in every nation where the distribution has taken the tracks, at every hour of every day. The working my enemies deployed against me has produced its own most effective counter-working. They pushed me into the season that produced the music. The music is now doing what no counter-working they could devise is capable of stopping.

That is what happens when the covenant is in operation and the Ruach is the source.

A Word Before We Move Forward

Everything in this chapter has been written to equip you — not to frighten you, not to create an obsessive awareness of spiritual threats, and not to suggest that the primary orientation of a covenant believer should be toward the enemy's tactics rather than toward the faithfulness of Yahuah. The primary orientation of a covenant believer should always be toward Yahuah — toward the blueprint He holds, toward the assignment He has commissioned, toward the promises He has spoken, and toward the Ruach He has given as both the seal and the guarantee of everything He has promised.

The knowledge of this chapter is supplementary to that orientation, not substitutive for it. You do not need to spend your days scanning your environment for color patterns and suspicious objects and directional circles. You need to spend your days in the presence of Yahuah, in the covenant that covers you, in the assignment He has given you, and in the worship that keeps the atmosphere around you saturated with His name and His presence.

But when something crosses your path that your spirit identifies as intentional and targeted — as mine did in that hotel lobby on the night a man walked a deliberate circle around my wife and me — you now have the vocabulary to name it, the authority to refuse it, and the covenant to stand on as you continue walking forward unbothered, unbound, and undefeated.

Because that is what the children of the covenant do.

They keep walking.

CHAPTER TWO

The Circle Walk

Recognizing the Enemy's Tactics in Real Time

"Be sober-minded. Be watchful. Your adversary the devil prowls around like a roaring lion, seeking someone to devour."

— 1 Kefa 5:8

In My Own Words — John Alan Legette

I want to tell you exactly what happened that night.

Not a generalized version. Not a spiritually sanitized retelling that smooths out the specific details in favor of a more comfortable narrative. The specific details are the testimony. The specific details are what make this account documentable, verifiable, and transferable to your own experience in ways that a vague spiritual story cannot be. So I am going to tell you exactly what I saw, exactly what I felt in my spirit, exactly what I did, and exactly what we found the next morning — because every single element of what happened that night is a vocabulary word in a language that the people who deployed it have been speaking for a very long time, and you deserve to be able to read that language as fluently as they write it.

My wife and I were in a hotel. We were traveling —
part of the unplanned evangelical tour that Yahuah had
orchestrated through the very circumstances our
enemies had set in motion to destroy us, which I will
tell you about in full in Chapter Six. We had checked
in, we were standing in the lobby area, and everything
about the moment was ordinary. Nothing in the visible
environment gave any indication that what was about to
happen was anything other than the routine activity of
other hotel guests going about their business.

And then a man began to move.

He had been standing with his family — his wife and
children were positioned behind us — and he moved
away from them toward the hotel counter. That
movement in itself was unremarkable. But then instead
of returning directly to where his family was standing,
he continued moving. He moved to the right of us. He
moved behind us. He completed a full circuit around
both my wife and me — a complete circle — and
returned to the position where he had started, near a
suitcase on the left side of where we were standing.

In the natural, to anyone watching without spiritual
awareness, this might have looked like a man who had
briefly lost track of where his luggage was and taken an
indirect path back to it. That was, in fact, exactly the
explanation he offered when I confronted him directly
— which I will get to in a moment. He claimed he
thought his wife had placed the suitcase to the right of
me, became confused, walked in that direction, and

then realized the suitcase was actually to the left where it had been all along.

But here is what my spirit registered the moment that circuit was completed.

Something is wrong with what just happened.

Not a vague sense of unease. Not a general spiritual discomfort. A specific, clear, internal recognition that what I had just witnessed was deliberate, was intentional, was targeted, and was not what it appeared to be on the surface. Yahuah had been sharpening my discernment through years of sustained spiritual opposition — and in that moment, that sharpened discernment activated with the clarity and the precision of an alarm system that has been properly calibrated for exactly this kind of intrusion.

I asked him directly. I turned to this man and I asked him why he had walked a circle around us.

What happened next was itself instructive.

He did not answer the question. He did not say — oh, I apologize, I realize that must have looked strange, let me explain. He did not engage with the question honestly or transparently the way an innocent person, surprised by an unexpected accusation, typically does. Instead he became agitated. He tried to make a scene. He escalated the interaction into a confrontation designed to make me look unreasonable for asking, to create enough social chaos and noise that the question itself would be buried under the distraction of the confrontation he was generating.

That response was the second confirmation. Innocent people answer questions. People who have been caught doing something they should not be doing create distractions.

His family, who had been standing behind us throughout, had apparently never checked in. They had no hotel room. They had no visible legitimate reason to be present in that lobby at that specific time. Shortly after the confrontation, they left. Not to a room. Out of the hotel entirely. The entire visit — the arrival, the circle walk, the scene, the departure — had the character of a group that came to that hotel with one specific purpose, executed that purpose, and left when the purpose was complete.

I stood there with my wife and I knew — with the settled, unfrightened, covenant-grounded clarity that Yahuah had been building in me through every difficult season that preceded that moment — that I had just witnessed an intentional spiritual working being performed against us in a hotel lobby.

And I also knew, with the same clarity, that it had not worked.

Not because I had done anything to stop it in the moment. But because the One whose covenant covered me had already addressed it before it was deployed, the same way He had addressed every other working that had been directed at me throughout this season of sustained opposition. The working hit the wall of the covenant and produced no fruit for the people who sent it.

What it did produce — as every attack against me has ultimately produced — was more testimony. More evidence. More documentation of the gap between what the enemy intends and what the covenant permits.

The next morning I would find out just how layered the working had been. But before I tell you what we found on that patio, let me teach you the ancient tradition that explains exactly what that man was doing when he walked that circle — because what he did has a name, a history, and a documented methodology that goes back centuries.

TEACHING: The Circle Walk — Ancient Traditions of Directional Magic and What They Mean

A Teaching for Every Believer Who Needs to Recognize Spiritual Tactics in Ordinary Settings

---

The Circle in Magical Tradition

The circle is perhaps the single most universally significant geometric form in the history of human spiritual practice. Across every culture, every era, and every continent, the circle has carried consistent spiritual meaning — it is the symbol of completion, of boundary, of contained power, and of the definition of sacred or cursed space. When a practitioner draws, walks, or traces a circle in a spiritual context, they are not making an aesthetic gesture. They are performing an act of spiritual architecture — defining the boundary of a field of intention and claiming the space within that boundary for a specific purpose.

In ceremonial magic traditions the circle is used to contain and protect the practitioner — drawn around themselves to keep external forces out and internal workings contained. But in folk magic traditions — particularly the Irish, Scottish, Celtic, Hoodoo, and conjure traditions that form the backbone of American folk magical practice — the circle is used in a fundamentally different way when walked around another person. Instead of containing the practitioner, it contains the target. The circle walked around another person is not a protective act for the walker. It is an enclosing act against the target — an act of claiming energetic territory around that person and sealing them within a field of the walker's intention.

This is a distinction of enormous practical significance. When someone walks a circle around you, they are not protecting themselves from you. They are attempting to enclose you within a working of their own creation and intention.

Deosil and Widdershins — The Two Directions of Power

The most critical technical element of circle walking magic is the direction of the walk, and this is where the tradition becomes both precise and ancient. Two terms from Scottish and Celtic magical tradition govern everything about the interpretation of a walked circle — deosil and widdershins.

Deosil, pronounced JEH-shul, means sunwise — clockwise, following the path of the sun across the sky from east to west through south. Walking deosil around a person, a place, or an object is associated across virtually every tradition that uses directional walking with blessing, healing, protection, attraction, and the invoking of positive and generative energy. The deosil walk follows the natural order of creation — the movement of the sun, the turning of the seasons, the direction of growth and flourishing. If someone walked deosil around you with genuine positive intention, the traditional understanding is that they were drawing protective energy toward you, sealing a blessing around you, or confirming a positive working in your life.

Widdershins, also spelled withershins, means the exact opposite — counterclockwise, moving against the sun. This direction is embedded in folk tradition as the direction of cursing, banishing, breaking, unraveling, and malevolent working. The widdershins walk moves against the natural order — it reverses the direction of growth, it opposes the movement of the sun, and in folk magical logic it therefore has the power to reverse, undo, bind, and bring misfortune upon whatever it encircles. Historical records from Scottish witchcraft trials of the sixteenth and seventeenth centuries document accused practitioners describing in specific detail how they walked widdershins around people or objects to place curses or initiate workings of harm. The tradition is not obscure. It is centuries old, cross-cultural, and extraordinarily consistent in its documentation.

In the folk magic tradition it was considered deeply unlucky — and in some traditions actively dangerous — to have someone walk widdershins around you. The walking itself was understood to initiate the working, and the completion of the circuit was understood to seal it. Three widdershins circuits around a person was one of the most cited formulas in British and Irish folk magic for placing a binding or a curse — the number three being considered magically potent enough to seal the intention permanently.

I am not in a position to tell you with certainty whether the man who walked that circle in the hotel lobby moved clockwise or counterclockwise. The specific direction was not something I was tracking in the moment because I had not yet fully developed the specific vocabulary around directional walking that I have since acquired through research and spiritual education. What I can tell you is that everything about the context — the hostile intent, the defensive escalation when confronted, the physical staging that followed overnight, and the layered nature of the overall working — is entirely consistent with a widdershins working rather than a deosil blessing.

People who are blessing you do not create scenes when asked why they are doing it.

Why It Can Be Done Without Your Knowledge

One of the most significant and most unsettling aspects of circle walking as a form of magical working is that it requires no visible tools, no spoken words, no ritual paraphernalia, and no ceremony that would be distinguishable to an outside observer from ordinary movement. All that is required is the physical act of walking the circle combined with focused intention. This means it can be performed in any ordinary setting — a hotel lobby, a grocery store, a church foyer, a public park, a workplace — and the only thing that distinguishes it from casual movement is the intention of the person doing the walking and the spiritual discernment of the person being walked around.

This is precisely why 1 Kefa 5:8 uses the specific imagery it uses. The adversary does not announce himself. He does not arrive with visible horns and a placard declaring his intentions. He prowls. He moves through ordinary spaces in ordinary appearing ways. He uses people who look like hotel guests, who travel with families, who carry suitcases and stand in lobbies and appear to be doing nothing more unusual than any other traveler in any other hotel on any other night.

The defense against an invisible weapon is not more sophisticated armor. It is the kind of spiritual alertness that Kefa describes — sober-minded, watchful, calibrated to the specific frequency of the adversary's movement patterns. That kind of alertness is not paranoia. It is the trained and disciplined watchfulness of a person who has been in spiritual conflict long enough to know what the adversary's footsteps sound like even when he is trying to walk quietly.

My spirit heard those footsteps in that lobby. And the confrontation that followed — uncomfortable as it was in the moment — was the right response. Not because confronting him broke the working. But because naming what you see is itself an act of covenant authority. When a covenant believer turns to the person attempting a working and says I see what you are doing — that declaration carries spiritual weight that the worker did not anticipate and cannot easily neutralize.

What a Binding Spell Through Circle Walking Is Designed to Do

The specific type of working most commonly associated with widdershins circle walking in folk magic tradition is the binding spell. Understanding what a binding spell is designed to accomplish is essential for understanding why someone would go to the trouble of sending a person to a hotel lobby specifically to walk one around a target.

A binding spell is not primarily a curse in the conventional sense — it is not designed to bring immediate visible misfortune upon the target, though that can be a component of it. It is designed to restrict. To freeze. To suppress. To prevent the target from acting, from advancing, from exercising their gifts and their authority, and from fulfilling the assignment that makes them a threat to the person deploying the working. The binding is specifically aimed at the target's capacity to move forward — their spiritual momentum, their creative output, their relationships, their influence, and their ability to operate effectively in their calling.

In the context of my situation this is particularly significant. The people pursuing me are not primarily trying to destroy me in an obvious, dramatic, immediately visible way. They are trying to stop me. They are trying to prevent me from advancing, from being heard, from producing the content and the ministry that has been flowing through me with increasing force and increasing reach. A binding working fits that objective precisely — it is designed not to wound but to freeze, not to kill but to contain, not to destroy but to suppress.

What they did not account for — what no binding working can account for when deployed against a covenant vessel — is the principle of Zechariah 4:6. A binding spell operates on human capability. It is designed to restrict what the target can do in their own strength, through their own resources, by their own effort. But when the source of what is flowing through a vessel is not the vessel's own strength but the Ruach of Yahuah — when the output is not produced by human capability but by divine anointing — the binding has nothing to bind. You cannot restrict what you cannot reach. You cannot freeze what is not operating in the dimension your working occupies. The Ruach moves where it will, through whatever vessel it chooses, at whatever rate it determines, and no folk magic binding deployed in a hotel lobby can follow it into the dimension where it operates.

The binding produced eighty two albums. The freeze produced five hundred and eighty nine teachings. The suppression produced the largest Hebrew Roots catalog in history.

Because the Ruach cannot be bound.

In My Own Words — What We Found the Next Morning

I want to return to my own voice now because what happened the next morning requires the specificity of firsthand account to carry its full weight.

I woke up the morning after the circle walk in the hotel lobby and went to look out through the patio door of our ground floor room. The room number was thirty five. The patio was directly adjacent to the area where we had slept — accessible from outside the hotel perimeter, visible through the glass of the patio door, and directly in the atmosphere of our sleeping space.

On the patio there was a muddy footprint.

Not a smudge. Not an ambiguous mark that could have been anything. A footprint — deliberate, visible, and positioned in a location that required someone to have come specifically to that patio rather than passing it incidentally. There was no pathway that would take a casual hotel guest past that specific patio in the course of ordinary movement. Someone had come to that patio. Someone had stood there. Someone had left a physical mark of their presence in the space immediately adjacent to where my wife and I had been sleeping.

And in one of the chairs on that patio there was a stick.

Not a stick that had blown in from a nearby tree. A stick that had been placed. Deliberately. In a chair. Positioned so that it was pointing — aimed — in the direction of the interior of our room, toward the window behind which we slept. It was situated with the specific intentionality of an object that had been arranged rather than deposited randomly. Its orientation was deliberate. Its placement in the chair rather than on the ground was deliberate. The direction it was pointing was deliberate.

Standing at that patio door in the morning light, looking at the footprint and the stick, I understood with complete clarity that what had begun in the lobby the previous evening had continued overnight. The circle walk in the lobby had been the opening move. The footprint and the stick on the patio were the follow-through — the physical staging of additional layers of the same comprehensive working, deployed while we slept.

And then I looked at the cars parked outside our room.

Approximately twelve vehicles were visible from our window. And their colors — distributed across those twelve vehicles in a pattern that spread liberally through the arrangement — were white, gray, blue, and black.

The exact combination we discussed in Chapter One.

I stood there, I looked at all of it, and I made a decision that I want you to understand was not the product of spiritual naivety or covenant presumption. It was the product of covenant knowledge applied with covenant authority. I decided that none of it had worked. I decided that whatever had been deployed against us through the circle walk, the footprint, the stick, and the color arrangement had encountered the wall of the covenant and had produced no fruit for the people who sent it. I decided to remove the physical objects, cleanse the space, declare the covenant over everything, and keep moving.

Because that is what the covenant empowers you to do.

TEACHING: Foot Track Magic, the Directed Stick, and Physical Staging — The Complete Vocabulary of What Was Deployed

A Teaching for Every Believer Who Needs to Understand What Physical Objects Mean in Folk Magic Tradition

Foot Track Magic — The Tradition Behind the Footprint

The muddy footprint on that patio was not an arbitrary element of what was deployed that night. It was a specific, deliberately executed component of one of the most extensively documented traditions in American folk magic — a practice known as foot track magic, sometimes called track tricks in the Hoodoo and conjure traditions.

The foundational principle of foot track magic is this — a person's footprint, the ground they walk on, and the physical traces of their movement through space carry a direct spiritual connection to that person. In folk magic tradition, gaining access to someone's track — the physical impression of their foot in earth or another surface — is considered equivalent to gaining access to the person themselves. Working the track is working the person. Laying something in a person's track — a prepared powder, a specific substance, an object charged with intention — is understood to attach that working directly to the person whose track it is, so that they carry it with them from that point forward with every step they take.

Applied to the sleeping space this principle becomes even more significant. Folk magic sources across multiple traditions are consistent on this point — the closer to a sleeping person's space a working is laid, the more potent it is considered to be. The sleeping person has their natural defenses lowered. Their spirit is at its most vulnerable. The space immediately surrounding where they sleep is the most intimate and most accessible spiritual territory associated with them. Gaining physical access to that space — standing in it, leaving a physical mark in it, depositing a physically staged working in it — is, in the logic of this tradition, the most direct and most effective means of attaching a working to a target.

Someone came to that patio while we slept and stood in the space immediately outside the window behind which we were resting. They left the physical mark of their presence. And in doing so, in the logic of the tradition they were operating in, they were laying a working in our track in the most intimate and most vulnerable space available to them.

The covenant response is Psalm 91:11-12 — *For He will command His angels concerning you, to guard you in all your ways. On their hands they will bear you up, lest you strike your foot against a stone.* The angels assigned to guard the ways of the covenant believer do not take nights off. They do not stand down because someone has approached the sleeping space of the person they are assigned to protect. The access that folk magic tradition considers spiritually significant — the access to the sleeping space, the track, the intimate territory of the resting person — is access that the angelic guard of the covenant does not permit to translate into effective spiritual harm against the protected person.

The footprint was real. The working was real in the sense that it was genuinely intended and genuinely deployed. The protection was more real than both.

The Directed Stick — The Spiritual Arrow

The stick positioned in the chair on that patio, pointed toward the window of our room, was not decoration and it was not debris. It was a spiritual arrow. In Hoodoo, conjure, and multiple folk magic traditions, sticks, bones, and wand-like objects placed pointing toward a person's home, bedroom, or sleeping area are used as directional anchors for a curse — objects charged with specific intention that are positioned to continuously direct that intention toward the target in the way that an arrow continuously points toward whatever it is aimed at.

The Wikipedia documentation on Hoodoo specifically references a walking stick found hidden inside the walls of the Bennehan house — placed there with the explicit purpose of continuously directing a curse at the family living within those walls. The stick does not need to be seen by the target to function in this tradition. Its power is not dependent on the target's awareness of it. It functions as a spiritual transmitter — a continuously broadcasting instrument of the practitioner's intention, aimed and left in position to keep directing the working toward its target.

The placement of the stick in the chair rather than simply on the ground is a detail that matters. Placing it in the chair elevated it — gave it a position, a deliberate orientation, a staged quality that ground placement would not have conveyed. It was set up as a directional instrument with specific aim. The chair was its mount. The window was its target. And the space where we slept was what the aim was locked onto.

Together with the footprint, the stick represented the completion of a three-part working deployed against us in that location — the circle walk in the lobby initiating the working and marking the target, the footprint in the sleeping space laying the working in our track at its most intimate point, and the directed stick maintaining continuous directional transmission of the working's intention toward us throughout the night and into the following day.

This is what practitioners call a compound working — multiple methods used in combination to ensure that the intention penetrates from multiple angles simultaneously and that the working holds its position against the target over an extended period rather than being a single event that dissipates.

The covenant response is Isaiah 54:17 — *No weapon formed against you shall prosper.* The weapon was formed. The weapon was positioned. The weapon was aimed. And it did not prosper. The evidence of that non-prosperity is documented in the pages of this book with numbers and timelines and a worldwide distribution infrastructure that was built in the months following that night by the vessel the weapon was aimed at.

The Color Arrangement — The Final Layer

The twelve vehicles outside our window in the specific color pattern of white, gray, blue, and black represented the final visible layer of the comprehensive working that had been deployed against us in that location.

As I explained in Chapter One, this specific color combination maps directly to a comprehensive offensive working designed to expose and strip away spiritual covering through white, create confusion and cloud discernment through gray, exploit emotional vulnerability through blue, and suppress, bind, and drive away through black. The distribution of these colors across approximately twelve vehicles in a pattern that spread liberally through the arrangement means the color field was not concentrated in a single point — it was spread across the entire visual field accessible from our room, so that wherever we looked through our window, we were looking at the color working.

Whether those specific vehicles were deliberately arranged by people coordinating with those who had staged the other elements of the working, or whether the color pattern was a natural result of the most statistically common car colors clustering in a particular parking lot on a particular night, the working in its totality — the circle walk, the footprint, the stick, and the color field — was comprehensive and intentional in its design even if not every element required direct physical coordination.

What I can tell you with certainty is that the combination of all four elements together, in that specific location, on that specific night, immediately following the identification of the circle walk in the lobby, and in the context of the broader sustained opposition that had been directed at me for an extended period by a coordinated group of people with the knowledge and the motivation to deploy exactly these kinds of workings — that combination did not present itself to my spirit as random coincidence.

It presented itself as a vocabulary. Written in the language of folk magic tradition. Addressed specifically to me and to my wife. And answered, definitively and completely, by the covenant.

TEACHING: Spiritual Discernment as Covenant Protection — The Lesson of That Night

A Teaching for Every Believer About the Power of Recognizing What Is Being Done

Of everything that happened on that night and that morning, the single most significant element was not the circle walk. It was not the footprint. It was not the stick or the color arrangement. The single most significant element was the fact that I recognized the circle walk as it was happening.

Not afterward. Not through research the following day. In the moment. While the circuit was still being completed.

That recognition — that immediate, specific, spiritually activated awareness that what I was witnessing was intentional and targeted — is itself a form of covenant protection that deserves to be examined as carefully as any of the physical tactics that were deployed against us. Because the folk magic tradition is consistent on this point — a working has far less power over a target who sees it clearly, names it out loud, and consciously refuses it, than over a target who is completely unaware of what is being done to them.

The power of an unseen working is partly the working itself and partly the unimpeded operation of the working in the spiritual atmosphere of an unaware target. When the target becomes aware — when they see it, name it, and stand against it from a position of covenant authority — they are not just resisting the working. They are actively dismantling the component of its power that depends on the target's unawareness. They are turning on the light in the room where the working was trying to operate in darkness.

This is the practical application of Hoshea 4:6 in real time. My people are destroyed for lack of knowledge. The inverse of that declaration is this — my people are protected by the presence of knowledge. The discernment to see what is happening, the knowledge to understand what it means, and the covenant authority to name it and refuse it are three layers of protection that work together to create a spiritual posture that is extraordinarily resistant to exactly the kind of targeted working that was deployed against us that night.

The sharpening of that discernment did not happen overnight. It was the product of years of sustained spiritual opposition during which Yahuah was calibrating my spiritual senses to the specific frequencies of the enemy's movement — teaching me through repeated exposure what the adversary's tactics look and feel like in real settings, with real people, in ordinary appearing circumstances. Every previous season of opposition had been a training exercise for the moment when I would need to recognize a circle walk in a hotel lobby and know immediately and accurately what I was looking at.

This is why the opposition that intended to destroy me has instead equipped me. Every attack sharpened a gift.

Every working refined a discernment. Every tactic I survived became a vocabulary word in a spiritual language that I can now teach to you — so that when you encounter similar patterns in your own experience, you have the knowledge, the authority, and the covenant to stand in.

What to Do When You Recognize It

If you are in a situation where your spirit alerts you — as mine did in that lobby — that something intentional and targeted is happening around you, here is the covenant posture to take immediately.

Do not react from fear. Fear is the goal of the working and fear is the condition under which the working has its greatest effectiveness. The adversary wants your fear response because fear activates a neurological and spiritual state that reduces clarity, increases vulnerability, and moves you away from the settled covenant authority that is your most effective defense. Breathe. Stand. Settle into the peace that surpasses understanding.

Do name what you see. Not loudly, not aggressively, but clearly and with authority. In your spirit, and where appropriate out loud, name what is happening and declare the covenant over it. I see what this is and I declare it null and void in the name of Yahshua HaMashaich. The declaration is not a formula — it is a covenant assertion. It is saying to the working, to the practitioner, and to every spiritual entity involved in its deployment — you have reached the boundary of the covenant and you cannot cross it.

Do remove and cleanse any physical components of the working that you have access to. The stick on the patio was removed. The area was cleansed with salt and prayer. The physical staging of the working was dismantled. This is not superstitious behavior — it is the covenant believer refusing to allow the physical instruments of a hostile working to remain in their space and continue functioning as directional anchors for the practitioner's intention.

Do continue moving forward. This is perhaps the most important practical instruction in this entire chapter. The goal of the working was to stop me. The most complete and most thorough refusal of that goal is to keep going. Every album that came out of that season was a step forward that the working had tried to prevent. Every teaching that went up on YouTube was forward momentum that the binding was designed to freeze. Every city reached on the evangelical tour was territory claimed in the name of Yahuah that the suppression working had tried to keep empty.

The most powerful response to a binding is to be found walking freely on the other side of it.

Which is exactly where I am.

The Night in Summary — What It All Means for You

The night I have described in this chapter — from the circle walk in the hotel lobby to the footprint and the stick on the patio to the color arrangement visible through our window — was a comprehensive, layered, multi-component spiritual working deployed against my wife and me by people with the knowledge, the motivation, and the coordination to execute it.

It did not work.

Not because I am exceptionally powerful. Not because my counter-measures were exceptionally sophisticated. Not because I happened to be in the right spiritual condition on that particular night. It did not work because of Numbers 23:23. Because of Isaiah 54:17. Because of Psalm 91. Because of the covenant that covers every child of Yahuah who is walking in their assignment under His authority and trusting His protection rather than their own capability.

The working was real. The intention behind it was genuine and hostile. The effort expended in its execution was significant — involving at minimum a family who traveled to that hotel specifically to execute the circle walk component, and at minimum one additional person who came to our patio overnight to stage the footprint and the stick. This was not a casual or incidental effort. It was a coordinated, multi-person, specifically targeted attack.

And it produced nothing for the people who sent it.

What it produced for me and for my wife was more testimony. More evidence. More documentation of the gap between what the enemy can deploy and what the covenant can withstand. More clarity about the nature of the opposition we were facing and the specific tactics being used. More sharpening of the discernment that would make every subsequent attack easier to recognize and more thoroughly refused.

They came to bind us. Yahuah used their coming to equip us.

By design. Not by chance.

Not even the attacks are random. Not even the opposition is outside the blueprint. Yahuah had already written the response to what they deployed before they deployed it, and the response he wrote was not our defeat. It was our testimony. It was this chapter. It was the knowledge you now carry into your own life and your own encounters with the enemy's tactics.

Take it with you.

Stand on the covenant.

Keep moving.

CHAPTER THREE

The Psychology of Obsession

Why the Enemy Cannot Stand to See You Walking in Peace

"But the wicked are like the troubled sea, when it cannot rest, whose waters cast up mire and dirt. There is no peace, says my Elohim, for the wicked."

— Yeshayahu 57:20-21

In My Own Words — John Alan Legette

There came a moment in the middle of everything I was walking through when I stopped and asked Yahuah a question that had nothing to do with strategy or protection or counter-working. It was a more fundamental question than any of those. It was the question that sits underneath all of the tactics and all of the opposition and all of the coordinated effort and asks — why?

Not why are they doing this in the sense of what are their methods. I had the answer to that question through research and through the spiritual discernment that Yahuah had been developing in me through years of sustained conflict. I understood the vocabulary of what was being deployed against me. I understood the traditions it was drawn from and the specific intentions each element was designed to accomplish.

The question I was asking was deeper than that.

Why does a person become so obsessed with another person's downfall that they are willing to recruit networks across multiple states, expend significant financial and spiritual resources, coordinate physical confrontations in hotel lobbies, stage overnight workings on hotel patios, and sustain a campaign of targeted opposition over an extended period of time against a single individual? What drives a human being to that place? What is happening inside a person that makes another person's continued existence in peace and purpose feel like an intolerable threat that must be eliminated at virtually any cost?

I sat with that question. I brought it before Yahuah. And as time passed and the full picture of the conflict came into clearer focus, the answer began to reveal itself — not all at once, but layer by layer, the way a complex architectural drawing reveals its full design as you study it from different angles and different distances.

What I found when I looked honestly and carefully at the people pursuing me was not what I expected to find. I expected to find hatred. What I found instead was something more fundamental and more tragic than hatred. I found the absence of peace. I found people who were so thoroughly lacking in genuine inner stillness, genuine security, and genuine contentment with their own lives and their own standing before

Yahuah, that the sight of me walking in the peace they did not possess had become genuinely intolerable to them. Not inconvenient. Not annoying. Intolerable — in the way that a bright light is intolerable to eyes that have spent too long in darkness.

My peace was not provoking them because I was doing anything aggressive toward them. My peace was provoking them because it was evidence of something they could not produce with all their resources, all their connections, all their craft, and all their power. It was evidence that there is a Source of stability, of purpose, of genuine rest, and of unshakeable forward momentum that exists entirely outside the systems they had built their lives and their identities around controlling.

And that evidence — walking around freely, producing music and teachings and books and ministry fruit at rates that defied every natural explanation, ascending higher with every passing month, refusing to be stopped by anything they deployed — was dismantling something in them that was more precious to them than anything else they possessed.

Their illusion of control.

I am going to spend this chapter unpacking what I discovered about the psychology of this kind of obsession — not to celebrate the suffering of the people who have pursued me, and not to build a case against them, but because what I learned about their condition is one of the most practically useful things I can share with you as a reader. Because if you are living out your calling with any degree of genuine faithfulness, there will come a time — if it has not already come — when someone in your sphere responds to your peace, your progress, and your anointing the way the people in my story have responded to mine.

And when that happens, you need to understand what you are actually looking at. Because misunderstanding the nature of the opposition leads to misunderstanding how to respond to it. And misunderstanding how to respond to it leads to wasted energy, unnecessary fear, and the diversion of your attention from the assignment that your peace is supposed to be protecting.

Let me show you what is actually happening when someone cannot stand to see you walking in peace.

TEACHING: The Psychology of Obsessive Opposition — What Drives a Person to This Place

A Teaching for Every Believer Who Has Ever Faced Inexplicable Hostility From People Who Have No Rational Reason to Oppose Them

---

The First Thing to Understand: It Is Almost Never Really About You

The most important and most liberating truth about the kind of obsessive, sustained, resource-intensive opposition described in this testimony is this — it almost never originates in anything the target actually did.

Read that again carefully because it runs counter to the natural human instinct to search your own behavior for the cause of the hostility directed at you. When someone pursues you with the level of coordinated, sustained, escalating effort that has been directed at me, the natural human response is to wonder what you did to provoke it. What mistake did you make? What boundary did you cross? What offense did you commit that justified this level of response?

The answer in cases like this is almost always — nothing that is proportional to what has been deployed against you. The opposition is not a measured response to a measured offense. It is a volcanic eruption from a pressure system that was building long before you appeared in the picture — and your appearance in the picture simply provided the trigger point at which the pressure found its outlet.

You are not the cause of the obsession. You are the occasion for it. There is a profound difference between those two things, and understanding that difference is essential for maintaining your spiritual equilibrium in the middle of a conflict whose intensity seems entirely disproportionate to anything you can identify as its origin.

What you actually did — in my case, inadvertently exposing people publicly whose power depends on the absence of exposure — was simply the trigger event. The obsession that erupted in response to that trigger was already present, already pressurized, already looking for a target. You provided the target. But the material that is fueling the obsession was deposited long before you arrived and will still be there, seeking another outlet, long after this particular conflict is resolved.

This does not make what is being done to you less real or less serious. It makes it more understandable. And understanding it accurately is the first step toward responding to it wisely.

Narcissistic Injury — The Wound That Produces Total War

The first and most foundational psychological dynamic driving the kind of obsession described in this testimony is what psychologists call narcissistic injury.

To understand this concept you first need to understand the specific psychological structure it belongs to.

A person with a narcissistic personality structure has built their entire sense of self — their identity, their security, their sense of worth and significance — on a carefully constructed and carefully maintained image of themselves as exceptional, powerful, superior, and beyond the reach of ordinary accountability. This image is not an honest self-assessment. It is a defensive structure erected to protect an interior world that is, in reality, profoundly fragile, deeply insecure, and terrified of exposure. The grandiosity is not confidence. It is a fortress built to keep the genuine self — the frightened, inadequate, unhealed self that lives beneath the performance — from being seen by others or even by the person themselves.

This structure functions reasonably well as long as the external environment cooperates with the image. As long as the people around the narcissistic person affirm, admire, comply, and do not challenge the constructed identity, the fortress holds and the person operates with the appearance of stability and authority. But the moment something penetrates the image — the moment someone challenges the narrative, refuses to comply, exposes something the image was concealing, or simply demonstrates by their existence that the narcissistic person is not the most powerful or the most significant presence in the room — the entire structure is threatened.

And the experience of that threat is what psychologists call narcissistic injury.

Narcissistic injury does not feel like ordinary embarrassment or ordinary criticism to the person experiencing it. It feels like annihilation. It feels like the complete destruction of everything they are — because the image is everything they are, in their own internal experience. When the image is threatened, the self is threatened. And the response to an existential threat — the response to the felt experience of being annihilated — is not measured, proportional, or governed by ordinary social restraint.

It is total war.

This is why the intensity of the opposition directed at me is so disproportionate to anything I actually did. I did not assault anyone. I did not commit fraud. I did not launch a campaign against them. I inadvertently exposed something they needed to keep hidden. In the real world, among healthy and accountable people, that kind of exposure — however uncomfortable — is something that can be addressed, explained, or moved past. But in the internal world of a narcissistically structured person, it is the worst thing that can happen. It is the unraveling of the fortress. It is the exposure of the frightened self beneath the performance. And the response to it — total, sustained, coordinated, escalating opposition directed at the person who caused the exposure — is entirely consistent with the psychological reality of what narcissistic injury feels like from the inside.

You did not provoke a measured response. You triggered a wounded ego's survival mechanism. And the wounded ego does not distinguish between what is proportional and what is not, because proportionality is a concept that requires the kind of self-awareness and other-awareness that the narcissistic injury state completely overwhelms.

Understanding this does not excuse what has been done. It explains it. And the explanation carries a specific kind of spiritual peace with it — because once you understand that what is being directed at you is the overflow of someone else's internal wound rather than a rational and proportional response to anything you actually did, you can stop carrying the weight of responsibility for it and stand in your covenant position with the clarity of someone who knows exactly what they are looking at.

Envy — The Oldest Spiritual Poison

The second dynamic driving this kind of obsession is envy — and envy must be carefully distinguished from jealousy because the distinction is critical for understanding what you are dealing with.

Jealousy wants what someone else has. It is painful and it is destructive, but at its core jealousy is about desire — the desire to possess what the other person possesses. Jealousy can theoretically be resolved by obtaining the desired thing, because the desire itself is the issue.

Envy is categorically different and categorically more destructive. Envy does not want what you have. Envy cannot tolerate that you have it at all. Envy looks at your peace, your anointing, your covenant covering, your forward momentum, your gifts, your purpose, your relationship with Yahuah — and instead of generating desire for those things in the envious person, it generates a burning, consuming need for those things to be taken from you. Not transferred to the envious person. Taken from you. Destroyed. Eliminated. So that the envious person does not have to look at evidence of what they do not possess and cannot produce.

This is the spirit that moved Cain against Abel. Abel had done nothing wrong. Abel had not taken anything from Cain. Abel had simply brought his offering and had it accepted — and that acceptance, that divine recognition and approval of Abel's offering, was more than Cain's envious internal state could tolerate. Not because Cain wanted Yahuah to accept his offering the way He accepted Abel's — but because he could not bear for Abel's offering to be accepted at all. The resolution envy demanded was not the elevation of Cain's offering. It was the elimination of Abel.

The people pursuing me are not pursuing me because they want what I have. They are pursuing me because they cannot tolerate that I have it. My covenant peace, my creative anointing, my forward momentum, my freedom from their control and their leverage — these things are not things they desire to possess. They are things they need to see destroyed, because their continued existence in my life is a continuous indictment of the emptiness and the futility of everything the people pursuing me have built their own lives around.

Every album that comes out is another indictment. Every teaching that goes up is another indictment. Every city reached on the evangelical tour is another indictment. Every morning I wake up still standing, still moving, still producing, still free — is another indictment. Not because I am trying to indict them. But because what I am and what flows through me in this season is the specific evidence of the specific reality that their entire system of power and control and occult practice cannot produce and cannot destroy.

That is envy in its purest and most destructive form. And it is exactly what Yeshayahu 57:20-21 describes — the wicked are like the troubled sea, when it cannot rest. The turmoil is not caused by you. The turmoil is their permanent internal condition. Your peace simply makes it visible by contrast.

The Substitution of Control for Inner Peace

The third dynamic is the one that perhaps most precisely explains the specific form the opposition has taken — the coordination, the recruitment, the elaborate workings, the sustained surveillance, the obsessive watching and investigating and attempting to prove fraud.

People who pursue power through occult practice, through the manipulation of others, through the construction of networks designed to enforce their will upon the world around them — these are almost universally people who have no genuine inner peace of their own. The pursuit of control is their substitute for peace. As long as they can manage outcomes, suppress threats, dominate their environment, and prevent anything from happening that they did not authorize and did not initiate — they can maintain the illusion of inner stability. The control is not peace. But it produces something that functions like peace from the outside — a kind of forced stillness that results not from genuine rest but from the suppression of everything that might disturb it.

The problem with control as a substitute for peace is that it requires constant maintenance. Genuine peace — the peace that Yahuah gives, the peace that surpasses understanding, the peace that is not dependent on circumstances or outcomes — requires nothing from the environment to sustain itself. It is self-generating because its source is inexhaustible. But control-as-peace requires that the environment keep cooperating. It requires that the threats keep being suppressed. It requires that the people who might disturb the forced stillness keep being managed, contained, and prevented from operating freely.

And I am the person in their environment who refuses to be managed, contained, or prevented from operating freely.

Every day that I continue moving forward — without their permission, without their resources, without their approval, and without being stopped by anything they have deployed against me — is a day that their control-as-peace is destabilized. Every album is a breach in the controlled environment. Every teaching is a gap in the containment. Every city reached is territory that their suppression working failed to hold. And as the breach grows wider and the gap grows larger and the territory expands beyond their reach, the desperate need to restore control becomes more consuming, more resource-intensive, and more detached from rational proportionality.

This is why the more they fail the bolder they get. This is why the opposition has escalated rather than diminished with every failed attempt. It is not the behavior of people who are winning. It is the behavior of people whose entire internal stability system is dependent on stopping something that they cannot stop — and who cannot afford, psychologically or spiritually, to accept that reality.

What the Obsession Actually Reveals About You

Here is the dimension of this teaching that I want you to receive with the full weight it deserves — because it is easy to read everything above and understand the psychology of the people pursuing you without understanding what that psychology reveals about you.

People do not mobilize this level of coordinated, sustained, multi-layered opposition against someone who is insignificant.

The scale of what has been deployed against me — the recruitment across multiple states, the coordinated workings, the physical staging, the sustained surveillance, the around the clock monitoring, the fraud investigation — all of this represents an extraordinary investment of time, energy, resources, and focus directed at a single individual. From a purely rational standpoint, this level of investment only makes sense if the return on not investing it — allowing the target to continue operating freely — represents an unacceptable threat to something the investing parties consider enormously valuable.

The obsession is therefore, in its own perverse way, a form of testimony about the significance of your assignment. You do not recruit covens across state lines to stop someone who poses no real threat to your power. You do not stage elaborate multi-component workings in hotel locations to bind someone whose gifts and calling represent no meaningful challenge to your agenda. You do not watch someone around the clock trying to prove they are a fraud if what they are producing does not genuinely frighten you.

The degree of the opposition is proportional to the degree of the threat. And the degree of the threat is proportional to the significance of the assignment.

This is entirely consistent with the pattern throughout the Hebrew scriptural record. The greater the calling, the greater the opposition. Joseph was not thrown into a pit and sold into slavery because he was ordinary. The pit and the slavery were the price of a calling that would eventually position him to preserve an entire generation. David was not hunted by Saul for years across the wilderness of Judah because he was inconsequential. The hunting was the price of a calling to the throne that would establish the covenant lineage through which the Messiah would eventually come. The prophets were not imprisoned and martyred because their words carried no weight. They were imprisoned and martyred because their words carried enough weight to threaten the power structures of entire nations.

Your enemies are your most inadvertent and most reliable witnesses to the significance of what Yahuah has placed in you. They would not be working this hard to stop something that did not matter. The very intensity of their effort is the testimony of your calling's magnitude.

Receive that understanding not with pride but with sobriety — because the same magnitude that makes the calling significant makes the responsibility of carrying it humbly and accountably before Yahuah absolutely critical. We will return to this in Chapter Five.

The Spiritual Diagnosis — Isaiah 57:20-21

Everything the psychology describes, the scripture diagnoses with more precision and more completeness than any clinical framework can achieve. Yeshayahu 57:20-21 is not a moral condemnation. It is a spiritual MRI — an image of the interior condition of the person who pursues another's destruction with this kind of obsessive, restless, sustained intensity.

The wicked are like the troubled sea, when it cannot rest, whose waters cast up mire and dirt. There is no peace, says my Elohim, for the wicked.

The image Yeshayahu uses is not of violence or of fire or of any of the conventional images of destructive force. It is the image of a sea that cannot rest. Water in constant, restless, churning agitation — not because anything from outside is disturbing it but because the agitation is its permanent internal condition. The sea does not choose to churn. It cannot stop churning. The turbulence is not an event in its experience — it is its experience. It is what the troubled sea is.

And what the churning produces — what rises to the surface from the depths of this permanent internal turbulence — is mire and dirt. Not creativity. Not beauty. Not anything constructive or generative or life-giving. The output of the troubled sea is the muck from its own depths, churned up and deposited on every surface it touches.

This is a precise description of the people who have pursued me and of the output of their campaign against me. The circle walk in the lobby. The footprint on the patio. The stick in the chair. The surveillance. The fraud investigation. The coordinated workings. None of this is creative, generative, or life-giving output. It is the mire and the dirt that churns up from a sea that cannot rest — the natural product of lives built on control and power and occult practice rather than on the covenant peace that only Yahuah can give.

And the declaration that closes the passage — there is no peace, says my Elohim, for the wicked — is not a threat. It is a statement of spiritual physics. The wicked do not have peace because the path they have chosen does not lead to peace. It cannot lead to peace. The control they pursue as a substitute for peace requires constant maintenance and produces constant anxiety. The power they accumulate as a substitute for security creates constant fear of losing it. The occult practice they employ as a substitute for covenant relationship keeps them in continuous engagement with spiritual forces that demand more than they give and leave the practitioner more depleted, more bound, and more restless with every working they perform.

There is no peace for them. Not as a punishment. As a consequence. As the inevitable and inescapable harvest of the seeds they have chosen to plant.

Contrast this with the verse that precedes it — Yeshayahu 57:19 — *Peace, peace to him who is far and to him who is near, says Yahuah, and I will heal him.* The peace that Yahuah speaks over His people is spoken twice — peace, peace — with the doubling that in Hebrew indicates completeness and emphasis. Not partial peace. Not conditional peace. Not peace that depends on the absence of opposition or the resolution of conflict. Complete, emphasized, covenant peace — available to those who are far and to those who are near, spoken by the One whose word does not return void.

The people pursuing me have no peace. I have peace, peace — the doubled, complete, covenant peace that Yahuah speaks over His children. And that asymmetry — my peace standing against their permanent agitation — is the dynamic that is driving everything described in this testimony. They cannot rest. I am resting. They are troubled. I am still. They are churning. I am ascending.

And the mire and the dirt they are casting up in their churning is landing not on my path but on their own shores.

The Pit Principle — Psalm 7:15-16

There is one final dimension of the spiritual diagnosis that deserves careful attention before we close this chapter, and it is found in Psalm 7:15-16.

He makes a pit, digging it out, and falls into the hole that he has made. His mischief returns upon his own head, and on his own skull his violence descends.

This is what the covenant calls the pit principle — the consistent scriptural teaching that the energy, the intention, and the effort that a person pours into the construction of harm directed at another person does not simply disappear when it fails to achieve its objective. It returns. It returns to its source. It returns with the accumulated force of everything that was invested in it and lands on the person who dug the pit rather than on the person the pit was dug for.

Consider the full inventory of what has been invested in the campaign against me. The financial resources. The time. The spiritual energy. The recruitment of networks. The coordination of workings. The physical staging. The sustained surveillance. The fraud investigation. The obsessive watching, analyzing, and attempting to disprove. All of that — every hour, every dollar, every spiritual resource, every ounce of occult energy deployed — was poured into a pit that was being dug for me. And the pit did not catch me. The covenant held. The protection was real. The weapons formed did not prosper.

Which means everything poured into that pit is still in it. And the person who dug it is standing at its edge.

I carry no satisfaction about this. I carry no desire for the people who have pursued me to fall. What I carry is the sober understanding that the spiritual law of Psalm 7:15-16 operates independently of my feelings about it and independently of my desire for it to activate or not activate. It operates the way gravity operates — not because anyone chose it, not because anyone wished it, but because it is the consistent and reliable nature of the spiritual physics that Yahuah built into the fabric of reality. The pit principle is not vengeance. It is consequence. And consequence does not require my participation or my endorsement to unfold.

My responsibility is not to push anyone into any pit. My responsibility is to keep walking forward in my assignment, trusting the covenant, and allowing the One who holds the blueprint to manage the outcomes for everyone involved in this story — including the people who have opposed me.

Because the blueprint was never only about me. It was about all of them too. And what Yahuah does with their story is His business in a way that I choose, consciously and deliberately, not to interfere with.

In My Own Words — What I Learned About Myself

The most important thing I want to tell you before we close this chapter is not about the people who have pursued me. It is about what looking at them closely and honestly taught me about myself.

There came a moment in the middle of processing everything I was witnessing — the obsession, the cruelty, the relentless escalation, the poor stewardship of power and influence — when I looked at all of it and I felt something that surprised me. Not contempt. Not satisfaction. Not vindication.

Fear.

Not fear of them. Fear of myself. Fear of what I could become.

Because what I was watching in the people pursuing me was not an alien species of human being. It was a recognizable human condition — pride unrestrained by accountability, power unmoored from humility, influence deployed in the service of self rather than surrendered to the purposes of Yahuah. And I recognized, with the sobering clarity of a person who has been given the specific and painful privilege of watching that condition in its fullest and most extreme expression, that the same seeds exist in every human heart. Including mine.

If I were to receive the promotion that Yahuah is bringing — the platform, the influence, the reach, the authority — and carry it without the daily governance of Yahuah, without the ongoing accountability to the covenant, without the consistent surrender of my will to His purpose — I could become a version of what I had been watching. Not the same version. Not executing the same specific tactics. But operating in the same essential spirit — using the influence I had been given to serve myself, to protect my image, to suppress challenges to my authority, to treat the people around me as instruments of my agenda rather than as beloved vessels of Yahuah deserving of honor and service.

That realization was one of the most important spiritual moments of this entire season. Not the music. Not the teachings. Not the ascending mountains or the arriving at Keystone. The moment when I looked at the worst example of corrupted power I had ever witnessed and said to Yahuah — that could be me. Keep me. Govern me. Hold me to the standard of the covenant in the season of abundance the same way You held me to it in the season of wilderness.

A person who can make that prayer honestly — and mean it — is a person who is safe to carry the authority of promotion. Because the prayer itself is the evidence that the pride that corrupts has not yet found a foothold in the soul of the one ascending.

This is why the people pursuing me failed the test that the season of their own elevation presented them with. Not because they were uniquely wicked or uniquely flawed. But because when their season of promotion came, they never looked at anyone else's corruption and said — that could be me. They looked at it and said — that could never be me. I am exceptional. I am above that. My power is too well-founded and my craft is too sophisticated for me to fall the way lesser people fall.

That assumption is the crack in every foundation that eventually brings the structure down.

I will not make that assumption. By the grace of Yahuah and the ongoing governance of His Ruach in my life — I will not make that assumption.

And the prayer I am making as I write this — the prayer I invite you to make as you read it — is this. Yahuah, show me what I could become without You. Show me clearly enough that I never stop needing You. And keep me in the posture of surrender that makes everything You have placed in me safe to carry and safe to release into the world.

That prayer is the armor that protects against the obsession described in this chapter. Not intellectual knowledge of narcissistic injury and envy and the substitution of control for peace — though that knowledge is genuinely valuable. The armor is the ongoing, daily, honest surrender to the One whose governance alone makes any of us trustworthy stewards of the gifts and the authority He places in our hands.

Keep walking. Stay humble. Stay surrendered.

And when you encounter the troubled sea that cannot rest — when someone's obsession with your downfall makes itself known in your life — remember what the sea's churning actually reveals.

It reveals that you have something it cannot produce and cannot destroy.

Walk in peace. Let them churn. The covenant holds.

CHAPTER FOUR

The Catalyst Principle

How Yahuah Uses Enemies as Instruments of Promotion

"You intended to harm me, but Elohim intended it for good, to accomplish what is now being done — the saving of many lives."

— Bereshit 50:20

In My Own Words — John Alan Legette

There is a question that every person who has endured sustained, coordinated, inexplicable opposition eventually asks. Not the tactical question of how to survive it. Not the strategic question of how to counter it. Not even the theological question of why Yahuah allows it. Those are important questions and this book addresses all of them. But there is a deeper question that lives underneath all of those — a question that only emerges after enough time has passed and enough of the full picture has come into view that you can begin to see the opposition not just as something you survived but as something that served a purpose you could not have anticipated when you were in the middle of it.

The question is this.

What was Yahuah actually doing while all of that was happening to me?

I asked that question. Not in desperation and not in accusation — I want to be clear about that because the posture from which you ask a question determines the kind of answer you are prepared to receive. I asked it with genuine curiosity, with the patient faith of someone who had already watched Yahuah move on his behalf in ways that were undeniable and specific and real time, and who had therefore established enough of a track record of divine faithfulness to be confident that if there was something being built in the middle of the difficulty, it was worth waiting to see what it was.

And as time passed — as the months of the sustained campaign against me accumulated, as the opposition escalated and I kept standing, as the gifts began to flow and the output began to accelerate and the full scope of what was being produced in this season came into view — the answer emerged with a clarity that was, in retrospect, almost embarrassing in its obviousness.

Yahuah was using them.

Not permitting them reluctantly while working around the damage they were causing. Not tolerating them as an unfortunate side effect of the spiritual conflict I was navigating. Using them. Actively. Purposefully. Sovereignly. With the same intentional precision that a master craftsman uses the specific tool that is most effective for the specific work being done at a specific phase of a specific project.

He was using the people who intended my destruction
as the instruments of my most significant preparation.
He was using their hostility, their coordination, their
sustained pressure, and their relentless escalation to
accomplish in me exactly what nothing comfortable,
nothing safe, nothing frictionless could ever have
produced — the specific, deep, tested, proven quality of
faith, discernment, surrender, and creative anointing
that the assignment ahead of me actually requires.

They thought they were destroying me.

They were graduating me.

This chapter is about the principle that makes that
possible — the principle I have come to call the catalyst
principle, which is the consistent and documented
pattern throughout the Hebrew scriptures and
throughout the experience of every covenant believer
who has walked this road before me, of Yahuah taking
what the enemy sends as a weapon and receiving it as a
tool, of taking what was intended as destruction and
converting it into the most effective instrument of
development and preparation available.

The chemistry of what happened to me. The theology
behind it. The practical application of it to your life.
That is what this chapter carries.

**TEACHING: The Catalyst Principle — What It Is
and How It Works**

The Chemistry of a Catalyst

The word catalyst comes from the Greek katalysis — meaning dissolution or loosing. In chemistry a catalyst is a substance that increases the rate of a chemical reaction without being consumed by the reaction itself. It does not create the elements that react. It does not add new material to the equation. It activates what is already present. It accelerates a reaction that the existing materials are capable of but that would occur far more slowly — or perhaps not at all under ordinary conditions — without the catalyst's presence.

This is a precise and illuminating description of what the opposition in my story has functioned as in my life. The faith was already present. The discernment was already deposited. The creative anointing, the teaching gift, the writing capacity, the ministry calling — all of these were already in me, placed there by Yahuah before the foundation of the world according to Ephesians 2:10. The opposition did not create any of them. It did not add anything to my spiritual constitution that was not already there.

What it did was catalyze them. It applied the precise conditions under which what was already present but dormant had to activate — had to come to the surface, had to become operational, had to flow at the rate and with the force and with the quality that the assignment ahead requires — because the alternative to activation under that pressure was not comfortable dormancy. The alternative was being overwhelmed by what was being thrown at me without the specific gifts and discernments and surrender that the pressure was designed to bring online.

Yahuah engineered the opposition to be the catalyst for exactly the activation He needed to occur in me before the next phase of the assignment could begin.

And here is the remarkable thing about a catalyst — it is not consumed by the reaction it accelerates. The opposition has been expending itself in the process of opposing me. Their resources, their time, their spiritual capital, their relationships — all of these are being consumed by the campaign they are running. But what the campaign has catalyzed in me — the faith, the discernment, the gifts, the anointing, the testimony — none of that is being consumed. It is being produced. It is accumulating. It is compounding with every passing month.

The catalyst is being spent. The reaction it triggered is producing something permanent.

The Joseph Template — The Most Complete Biblical Illustration

The most complete and most carefully documented illustration of the catalyst principle in the entire Hebrew scriptural record is the story of Joseph — and the parallels between his experience and mine are specific enough and consistent enough that I want to walk through them in some detail, because the Joseph template is not just an inspiring historical story. It is a structural blueprint that Yahuah has been following in the lives of His servants across generations, and understanding it specifically and precisely is one of the most practically useful things a believer in sustained opposition can do.

Joseph was the son of promise — the child born to Jacob and Rachel after years of barrenness, the child who carried from birth the specific sense of divine calling and elevated destiny that his father recognized and marked with the famous coat of many colors. He had genuine gifts — the prophetic dream capacity that manifested in the two dreams of his youth, the administrative intelligence that would eventually make him indispensable to every authority he served under. He had the calling. He had the gifts. He had the covenant covering of the Elohim of his fathers.

And then his brothers threw him in a pit.

Not because he had done anything wrong. Not because he had committed any offense proportional to what was done to him. Because his calling made them envious — the same dynamic we examined in Chapter Three. His coat, his dreams, his father's favor, the specific quality of divine marking on his life that they could see but could not replicate — these things produced in his brothers the same intolerable envy that my anointing and my peace and my forward momentum have produced in the people who have pursued me. And envy, when it has sufficient motivation and sufficient access, acts.

The pit was the beginning of thirteen years of preparation that Joseph could not see as preparation while he was in it. From the pit he was sold to Potiphar's household. In Potiphar's household he was falsely accused and imprisoned. In prison he was forgotten by the man whose dream he had accurately interpreted. Pit, slavery, false accusation, imprisonment, forgotten — thirteen years of what looked from every external angle like the progressive destruction of a man whose calling had promised something entirely different.

But here is what was happening in those thirteen years that the external angle could not see. Joseph was being educated in every dimension of Egyptian culture, administration, and power structure from the inside — not as a student but as a participant, learning how the most sophisticated civilization of his era actually operated at every level from household management to national governance. He was being tested under the specific condition that reveals more about a person's character than any other — the condition of unjust suffering, where the response to being wronged determines whether the gifts and the calling can be trusted with the authority they are destined to carry. He was being kept in the precise proximity to the precise people — Pharaoh's chief butler, Pharaoh's chief baker, ultimately Pharaoh himself — that his specific assignment required, through a series of events that no human strategic planning could have engineered and that made no sense in sequence until the final destination revealed what every step had been building toward.

And then Pharaoh had a dream.

And in one conversation — one divinely orchestrated, covenant-activated, assignment-fulfilling conversation — everything that had been building for thirteen years was installed at the apex. Joseph went from the prison to the palace in a single day. Not gradually. Not incrementally. Instantaneously. Because the preparation was complete. Because the foundation had been properly laid. Because every stone of the arch had been set in place from both sides during those thirteen years of what looked like destruction. And when the keystone moment arrived, the structure was ready to receive it and the weight it was designed to carry came immediately and completely.

Bereshit 50:20 is Joseph's retrospective declaration about the entire arc of what happened to him — *You intended to harm me, but Elohim intended it for good.* This is not a pious platitude offered from a safe distance from the pain of what was done to him. This is a man who has lived through the pit and the slavery and the false accusation and the imprisonment and the forgotten years, who has arrived on the other side of all of it, who has seen the complete picture, and who is declaring with the full authority of someone who actually knows what he is talking about — every single harmful thing that was done to me was received by

Yahuah as raw material for something He had already decided to build.

The brothers intended harm. Yahuah intended good. The same events. The same pit. The same sale. The same prison. Two entirely different intentions operating simultaneously on the same set of facts — and the intention of Yahuah was not merely equal to the intention of the brothers. It was sovereign over it. It took the brothers' intention, redirected its energy, and used it to accomplish something the brothers' intention was specifically designed to prevent.

That is the catalyst principle operating at its fullest and most complete expression. And it is exactly what has been operating in my life throughout this season of sustained opposition.

The Moses Parallel — Learning What Cannot Be Learned in the Palace

The second great biblical illustration of the catalyst principle is Moses — and the Moses parallel is particularly personal and particularly precise for me because of the specific nature of my own wilderness season and what it produced.

Moses at forty was a man of maximum human capability. Egyptian palace education, Egyptian military training, Egyptian administrative formation — the full toolkit of the most powerful human civilization of his era, applied to a man who also carried the blood of the covenant people in his veins and the awareness of their suffering in his heart. He had the calling — the awareness that Yahuah had something specific for him to do in relation to his people's deliverance. He had the capability — the tools and the formation and the position and the resources. He had the passion — the genuine burning desire to see his people free.

And he failed catastrophically on his first attempt. Not because the calling was wrong. Not because the passion was misdirected. But because the attempt was made in human might and human power rather than in the Ruach of Yahuah. The Egyptian toolkit was not the right toolkit for a divine assignment. The palace formation was not the right formation for covenant leadership. The human strategic plan — intervene in a single incident of injustice, demonstrate capability and willingness, galvanize the people around the moment — was not the right plan for delivering an entire nation from the most powerful political and military structure in the world.

The failure, the flight, the forty years in the wilderness — these are the catalyst. Forty years of tending sheep in Midian did something to Moses that forty years in Pharaoh's palace could never have done. It emptied him. It removed the Egyptian formation as his primary identity and his primary source of capability. It replaced institutional power with personal dependency on Yahuah. It replaced human strategic planning with the capacity to hear a voice from a burning bush and obey it even when what it asked made no sense through the lens of any Egyptian strategic framework.

Moses at eighty was not a more capable version of Moses at forty. He was a fundamentally different kind of vessel — one whose Egyptian formation had been replaced by wilderness formation, whose self-sufficiency had been replaced by surrender, and whose toolkit was no longer the toolkit of a palace but the toolkit of a covenant — a staff, a word from Yahuah, and the absolute certainty that the outcome did not depend on his capability but on the faithfulness of the One who commissioned him.

What the wilderness catalyzed in Moses was not achievable through any other means. The palace could produce capability. Only the wilderness could produce the specific quality of emptied, surrendered, Ruach-dependent character that the Exodus assignment actually required. The forty years were not a detour from the assignment. They were the specific preparation without which the assignment could not have been executed.

My thirteen years of homelessness and my eighteen years of creative drought are my wilderness. Not identical to Moses's in their specific content or their specific duration. But identical in their function — the systematic removal of reliance on human capability, human stability, and human resources as the foundation for the assignment, and the replacement of those things with a quality of surrender and dependence on Yahuah that produces output the wilderness shepherd rather than the palace prince can carry.

Moses at forty with all of Egypt's resources could not deliver Israel. John Alan Legette with conventional stability, conventional resources, and conventional creative capability could not have produced eighty two albums and five hundred and eighty nine teachings and the largest Hebrew Roots catalog in history. In both cases the assignment required the wilderness to empty out what the palace had deposited — so that what came out when the gates finally opened was the Ruach rather than the capability, the anointing rather than the talent, the covenant rather than the strategy.

The catalyst did its work. The wilderness did its work. And the output — in both cases — was not proportional to the human capacity of the vessel. It was proportional to the faithfulness of the Source flowing through a vessel that had finally been emptied enough to carry it.

The Specific Gifts the Catalyst Produced

I want to be specific about what the sustained opposition actually produced in me — because the principle is more useful to you as a reader when it is grounded in concrete specificity rather than kept at the level of general spiritual encouragement.

The first gift the catalyst sharpened was faith. Not the general agreement that Yahuah exists and is good — that kind of faith is accessible without difficulty and without cost. The specific, tested, proven, unshakeable quality of faith that comes from watching Yahuah intervene with specific strategies in specific situations against specific and formidable opposition — that quality of faith is only produced under the conditions that produce it. I have watched Yahuah dismantle coordinated plans sometimes before they were fully deployed, sometimes in the middle of their execution, and sometimes after the fact in ways that reversed the effects of what had already landed. Each instance added a layer to the foundation of faith that no teaching, no study, no comfortable season of ministry could have built. The faith I carry now is not theoretical. It has been load tested under conditions that would have collapsed anything built on a lesser foundation. And it held.

The second gift the catalyst sharpened was discernment — the specific, calibrated, real time spiritual perception that activated in that hotel lobby when a man walked a circle around my wife and me and my spirit knew immediately and accurately what it was witnessing. Discernment is not a gift that develops in the absence of what it is designed to discern. You cannot develop the ability to recognize spiritual attack without being under spiritual attack. You cannot develop the ability to identify the enemy's tactics without encountering those tactics in real settings with real consequences. Every working that was deployed against me — every circle walk, every physical staging, every coordinated effort — was simultaneously an attack and a training exercise. The attack was intended to harm me. The training exercise was intended by Yahuah to sharpen in me the specific spiritual perception that would make me increasingly effective at recognizing, naming, and refusing exactly these kinds of workings — not just for myself but for everyone I teach and minister to going forward.

The third gift the catalyst unearthed was the creative anointing — and this is the one that most visibly and most dramatically defies natural explanation. Eighteen years of creative silence. And then, in the season of the most intense sustained opposition I had ever experienced, the oil began to flow. Eighty two albums. One thousand one hundred and eighty tracks. Five hundred and eighty nine teachings. Eight books. None of this was produced by my natural creative capability developing gradually through practice and refinement. It erupted — suddenly, completely, at a rate that has no human precedent in the Hebrew Roots movement — because the opposition created the precise conditions of surrender and desperation and dependency on Yahuah under which a gift that had been deposited in me before the foundation of the world finally had a vessel available to flow through.

The catalyst did not create the gift. The gift was always there. The catalyst created the conditions under which the gift had no choice but to emerge — because the alternative to emergence was being overwhelmed by what was being thrown at me without the specific anointing that the assignment requires.

The fourth gift the catalyst produced was strategic spiritual intelligence — the specific capacity to receive from Yahuah strategies that dismantled enemy plans sometimes before they were deployed, sometimes during their execution, and sometimes after the fact in ways that reversed their intended effects. This is the gift described in Ephesians 6 as the full armor of Elohim — not passive protection but active, strategic, spiritually intelligent engagement with what is being directed against you. I could not have developed this capacity in the absence of opposition that required it. The strategy comes from Yahuah, but the vessel has to be developed to the point of being able to receive and implement it — and that development only happens in the conditions that require it.

Every gift that emerged in this season was always in me. The catalyst brought it out.

What This Means for the People Who Catalyzed It

There is a dimension of the catalyst principle that carries a specific kind of spiritual weight that I want to address honestly before we close this chapter — the dimension that concerns the people who served as the catalyst.

They did not intend to serve as a catalyst. They intended to serve as destroyers. The circle walk was intended to bind, not to activate. The sustained opposition was intended to suppress, not to sharpen. The being thrown out of our home was intended to destabilize, not to launch. Every element of the campaign against me was designed and deployed with the explicit intention of stopping what Yahuah had put in motion — and every element has instead accelerated it.

This is the profound and almost unbearable irony of the position they are in. They have been the most productive contributors to the very thing they have been trying to prevent. The national platform they tried to silence — they built it by throwing me out of my home and sending me on a tour across the country. The music catalog they tried to bind — they triggered its release by creating the precise conditions of surrender under which eighteen years of compressed anointing erupted. The worldwide distribution they tried to contain — they funded it by keeping me in the conditions of homelessness and displacement that kept me fully dependent on Yahuah as my sole source and therefore fully available to Him as an unimpeded vessel.

They are the most reluctant, most unwilling, most aggressively resistant ministry partners in the history of my calling. And Yahuah has been using them the entire time.

I do not say this to mock them. I say it because there is a lesson in their position that applies to every believer who has ever been the instrument of opposition against another covenant believer — whether they knew it or not. The scripture is clear and consistent on this point. What you send against a covenant person under the protection of Yahuah does not simply fail to achieve its objective. It is redirected. It is repurposed. It is turned back on itself in ways that serve the very assignment it was attempting to destroy. You cannot send a weapon against a covenant person without that weapon eventually becoming testimony for the covenant you tried to violate.

This is Yahuah's sovereign sense of irony in operation — and it is one of the most consistent and most beautiful patterns in the entire history of His dealings with His people and their enemies.

The Unearthing of Hidden Gifts — A Word Specifically for You

Before we close this chapter I want to speak directly to you — to the reader who is in the middle of sustained opposition right now and who cannot yet see what is being produced by what they are going through.

The gifts that are being unearthed in you through this season are not new gifts that the opposition is creating. They were placed in you before the foundation of the world, deposited by Yahuah for the precise moment and the precise assignment that your life is building toward. The opposition is not creating what is emerging in you. It is creating the conditions under which what was always in you has to come to the surface — because the surface pressure has exceeded the depth at which the gift could remain dormant.

You cannot discover that you have the gift of standing under sustained spiritual attack until you have been under sustained spiritual attack. You cannot discover the depth of your faith until your faith has been tested at a depth that exceeds what you thought you could bear. You cannot discover strategic spiritual intelligence until you are in a situation that requires it desperately enough that you cry out to Yahuah for it and He answers with something specific and effective and undeniably beyond your own natural strategic capacity.

Every gift that emerges in you through this season is a gift that was always there — waiting for exactly the conditions the opposition has created to bring it to the surface. The people pursuing you did not know they were functioning as the key that unlocks what Yahuah deposited in you before you were born. But that is exactly what they have been doing. And what they have unlocked will still be active, still flowing, still producing fruit in your life and in the lives of everyone your ministry touches long after the opposition that unlocked it has been forgotten.

They meant it for harm. Yahuah meant it for good.

That is not a cliche. In the lives of His covenant people it is a documented, testified, mathematically verifiable reality.

Your season of catalysis is producing something. You may not be able to see it yet from where you are standing in the middle of it. But it is being produced. The reaction is underway. The gifts are being activated. The faith is being tested and proven. The discernment is being calibrated. The surrender is deepening. The vessel is being emptied of everything that competes with the Ruach for control of the output.

And when the appointed time comes — when the preparation is complete and the catalyst has done the specific work it was designed to do — what comes out will not trickle. It will pour. Because eighteen years of compression does not produce a trickle. It produces the force of everything that was held back for all of that time, released in the moment the gates finally open.

Keep standing. The catalyst is doing its work.

And Yahuah is watching every reaction it produces.

In My Own Words — The Moment I Understood

I want to close this chapter in my own voice because the moment I fully understood the catalyst principle was not an intellectual moment. It was a worship moment.

I was in the middle of recording — somewhere in the flow of what has now become eighty two albums — and I stopped. Not because I was tired. Because something in me needed to stop and acknowledge what was actually happening. I sat with the music I had just produced and I thought about the people who had thrown me out of my home. I thought about the circle walk in the hotel lobby. I thought about the footprint on the patio and the stick in the chair and all of the coordinated effort that had been deployed against me over the extended period of this conflict.

And I laughed. Not bitterly. Not sarcastically. With genuine, covenant-grounded, spiritually illuminated joy. Because I could see it. I could see the full picture clearly enough in that moment to understand what it looked like from Yahuah's perspective — this army of people who had invested everything they had in stopping something they were simultaneously and unknowingly building. This elaborate, well-resourced, carefully coordinated campaign of destruction that had, step by step and decision by decision, catalyzed the largest Hebrew Roots music catalog in history.

They built what they were trying to destroy.

And in that moment of laughter and worship and genuine gratitude — including, I will confess, genuine gratitude for the people who had done their level best to destroy me — I understood Bereshit 50:20 not as a theological concept but as a personal reality. Not as something Joseph said about his brothers from a historical distance. As something I was saying about my own adversaries from the living, breathing, documented, musically recorded, globally distributed present tense of my own testimony.

You intended harm. Yahuah intended good. And the good He intended is already in the world — in every track, in every teaching, in every city that heard the sacred names because you threw me out of my home and gave me a national tour. The good is already in the world. The harm produced nothing that lasts.

That is the catalyst principle in its fullest expression.

That is what Yahuah does with the worst thing the enemy can send.

He turns it into worship.

CHAPTER FIVE

Poor Stewards of Power

What Corrupt Authority Reveals About Itself

"But Yahuah said to Samuel, 'Do not look at his appearance or at his physical stature, because I have refused him. For Yahuah does not see as man sees. For man looks at the outward appearance, but Yahuah looks at the heart.'"

— 1 Shemu'el 16:7

In My Own Words — John Alan Legette

I want to tell you about a question I asked Yahuah that changed the way I understood everything that was happening to me.

It was not a question about strategy. It was not a question about protection or about the specific tactics being deployed against me or about how to counter what was coming. Those questions had their place and Yahuah answered them with the specific, real time strategies that dismantled plan after plan before they could fully land. But this question was different. This question came from a place deeper than strategy. It came from the place where a person who has been watching something deeply painful and deeply wrong for an extended period of time finally has to ask not just what is happening but why — and not just why in the tactical sense but why in the theological and human sense.

The question was this.

Why did I have to meet these people?

I did not ask it in anger. I did not ask it in the desperate tone of someone looking for comfort in the middle of pain. I asked it with the genuine curiosity of someone who had already seen enough of Yahuah's sovereign orchestration of difficult circumstances to believe that the answer, when it came, would be worth the waiting. I asked it and then I did something that is harder than asking — I waited. I watched. I continued walking through the season without demanding an immediate answer, trusting that the full picture would reveal itself in Yahuah's timing rather than mine.

And as the months passed and the full arc of the conflict came into clearer view, the answer began to emerge with a clarity that was both illuminating and sobering.

Yahuah allowed me to meet these people before my divine promotion — specifically, deliberately, and with precise intentionality — to show me something I could not have seen any other way. He showed me what is in the hearts of people who are lifted up in pride. He showed me what power looks like when it is divorced from humility, from accountability, from genuine covenant relationship with the Most High. He showed me the full fruit of influence deployed in the service of self rather than surrendered to the purposes of Yahuah — the cruelty it produces, the obsession it generates, the destruction it causes to everyone who comes within its reach, and ultimately the self-destruction it visits upon the one who wields it.

He showed me all of that so that when the season of my own promotion arrived — when the platform expanded, when the influence grew, when the reach of what was flowing through me extended to nations and peoples I had never personally encountered — I would carry into that season a vivid, experiential, impossible-to-forget understanding of what I must never become.

The people who pursued me were not just my adversaries. They were my instructors. The most expensive, most comprehensive, most viscerally effective course in the stewardship of power and influence that anyone has ever been enrolled in — and Yahuah enrolled me in it specifically because of what was coming next in my story and because of what I would need to know when it arrived.

This chapter is about what I learned in that course. About what power reveals when it is poorly stewarded. About the amplification principle that makes the condition of a person's character the most important factor in determining whether the authority they carry becomes a gift to the world or a weapon against it. And about the most important question I turned on myself in the middle of everything I was witnessing — the question that I believe is the single most critical safeguard available to anyone who is being prepared for significant promotion and significant influence.

That question is not about the people who pursued me.

It is about me.

TEACHING: The Stewardship of Power — What Corrupt Authority Reveals and What It Requires

A Teaching for Every Believer Who Is Being Prepared for Promotion and Needs to Understand What That Promotion Will Require of Them

---

The Amplification Principle — Power Reveals, It Does Not Create

The most important thing to understand about power and influence is something that popular culture consistently gets wrong. The conventional wisdom is that power corrupts — that ordinary, decent people are transformed by the acquisition of power into something darker and more dangerous than they were before the power arrived. This framing locates the problem in the power itself — as though power is a corrupting substance that contaminates whatever vessel it enters, regardless of the initial condition of that vessel.

The scriptural record and the consistent evidence of human history tell a different and more precise story. Power does not corrupt. Power reveals.

Power is an amplifier. It takes whatever is already present in the character of the person who holds it and multiplies it. It removes the natural restraints that limited resources and limited influence impose on what a person is able to express and act upon in the world. It gives the internal condition of the person — their values, their priorities, their relationship to truth and to other people, the orientation of their will — a much larger platform for expression than that condition previously had access to.

A person who is humble, accountable, genuinely oriented toward serving others, and governed by a standard higher than their own judgment will use increasing power to increasingly serve, protect, and elevate the people around them. The power amplifies the humility. It amplifies the accountability. It amplifies the orientation toward others. And the result is authority that is genuinely safe to be near — authority that builds rather than destroys, that elevates rather than suppresses, that releases rather than controls.

A person who is insecure, prideful, self-serving, and unaccountable to any standard above their own will use increasing power to increasingly control, suppress, manipulate, and destroy. Not because the power changed them. Because the power removed the limitations that were previously keeping what was already in them from finding its fullest expression. The cruelty was always there. The manipulation was always present. The need to dominate and the inability to tolerate genuine challenge or genuine accountability —

these were features of the character before the power arrived. The power simply gave those features a larger stage and removed the practical constraints that had previously kept them from operating at their fullest and most destructive scale.

This is what I witnessed in the people who pursued me. Their poverty of character was not created by their power and influence. Their poverty of character was always present. What their power and influence did was remove every natural restraint that limited resources and limited social position had previously imposed on the expression of what was already in their hearts. What they were capable of doing to me — the coordination, the workings, the physical confrontations, the sustained surveillance, the recruitment of networks across the country — all of that required resources. Without the resources, the same impulses toward control and destruction would have been present but would have been practically constrained. With the resources, the impulses found their fullest possible expression.

This is why I said in the conversation that birthed this book — if they were poor, they could never have gone as far as they have. That statement is not about the morality of poverty or wealth. It is about the amplification principle. Their wealth and influence amplified what was already in their hearts. And what was already in their hearts, when fully resourced and fully expressed, produced the campaign described in this testimony.

The Heart Condition as the Governing Variable

First Shemu'el 16:7 gives us the foundational principle that governs everything the amplification principle implies. When Yahuah sent Samuel to anoint the next king of Israel, Samuel's natural human assessment focused on the outward appearance — the physical stature, the visible impressiveness, the conventional markers of leadership capability and authority. And Yahuah interrupted that assessment with a declaration that is one of the most important statements in the entire scriptural record about the nature of genuine authority.

Yahuah does not see as man sees. Man looks at the outward appearance. Yahuah looks at the heart.

The heart is the governing variable. Not the capability. Not the resource base. Not the network of relationships. Not the accumulated power and influence. Not the spiritual practices or the esoteric knowledge or the occult mastery. The heart. The internal condition of the person — their actual relationship to truth, to accountability, to the people around them, and to Yahuah Himself — is what determines whether the authority they carry will be used in ways that serve the purposes of Yahuah or in ways that serve the purposes of the self.

The people pursuing me have significant power. They have significant influence. They have significant resources and significant networks and significant knowledge of spiritual practices both conventional and occult. By every external measure of capability and authority, they are formidable. Yahuah looks past all of that and looks at the heart. And what He sees in the heart — the pride, the insecurity, the need for control, the absence of genuine accountability, the willingness to destroy lives for self-gain — is what determines His assessment of their authority and His response to the conflict between their agenda and the covenant He has established over my life.

The heart condition is what Saul failed and David passed. Saul had everything externally — the physical stature, the popular affirmation, the military capability, the institutional position. What he lacked was the heart condition that makes authority safe to carry. His insecurity, his pride, his inability to tolerate genuine challenge to his position, his willingness to sacrifice covenant relationship with Yahuah on the altar of his own image — these were the features of his heart that his kingship amplified rather than corrected. And the amplified expression of those features produced one of the most tragic stories in the entire Hebrew scriptural record — a man who was given everything and lost everything because what was in his heart was not fit to carry what his position required.

David, by contrast, carried genuine and profound failures of his own — failures that the scriptural record does not conceal or minimize. But the heart condition that distinguished him from Saul was not the absence of failure. It was the orientation toward Yahuah as his ultimate reference point and his ultimate authority even in the middle of his failures. When confronted with his sin, David did not deflect, did not attack the messenger, did not construct an alternative narrative to protect his image. He said — I have sinned against Yahuah. The accountability was real. The orientation was genuine. And that heart condition — that fundamental posture of genuine accountability to a standard higher than his own judgment — was what Yahuah identified as the governing variable when He called David a man after His own heart.

Not a man without failure. A man whose heart, in its deepest orientation, was pointed toward Yahuah rather than toward himself.

That is the heart condition that makes authority safe. And it is the heart condition that I am committed — consciously, deliberately, and with the full awareness of what I witnessed in the people who pursued me — to maintaining as the defining feature of how I carry whatever authority and influence Yahuah is bringing into my hands.

The Nebuchadnezzar Warning — What Happens When the Heart Condition Is Not Maintained

The most dramatic and most sobering illustration in the Hebrew scriptural record of what happens when a person in a position of significant power and influence fails to maintain the heart condition that makes that authority safe to carry is the account of Nebuchadnezzar in the book of Daniel.

Nebuchadnezzar was, by any measure of human authority and human achievement, one of the most powerful individuals who has ever lived. He ruled the most dominant empire of his era. He commanded armies that no other military force of his time could effectively challenge. He built structures — including the hanging gardens — that were considered among the wonders of the ancient world. He possessed resources, influence, and reach that made him the functional apex of human power in his generation.

And in Daniel 4, walking on the roof of his palace in Babylon, surveying the city that his power had built, he said the words that triggered one of the most dramatic divine interventions in the entire scriptural record.

Is not this great Babylon, that I have built for a royal dwelling by my mighty power and for the honor of my majesty?

The I. The my. The for my majesty. The complete absence from that declaration of any acknowledgment of the Source from whom every gift, every resource, every capability, and every achievement had come. The complete internalization of the credit for everything that had been produced — the attribution of the building to his power rather than to the One who had placed him in the position from which the building was possible.

The voice from heaven came immediately. The judgment was executed immediately. And for seven years Nebuchadnezzar lived as an animal in the field —

not as a punishment designed to humiliate him for its own sake but as the specific and precisely calibrated correction that would accomplish in him what no comfortable circumstance and no human accountability structure had been able to produce. The stripping of everything human — reason, dignity, social position, the ability to even process reality as a human being does — was the only intervention sufficient to break through the fortress of pride that had been constructed around a heart that had lost its genuine orientation toward the Source of all authority.

And then — and this is the part of the Nebuchadnezzar account that carries the greatest weight for this chapter — at the end of the seven years, Nebuchadnezzar lifted his eyes toward heaven. And his reason returned to him. And the first thing he did with his restored reason was declare what he had refused to declare before the judgment came.

I blessed the Most High and I praised and honored Him who lives forever. For His dominion is an everlasting dominion and His kingdom is from generation to generation.

The heart condition was restored. The orientation was corrected. The I and the my and the for my majesty were replaced with the acknowledgment of the One who is actually sovereign over all authority, all power, and all achievement. And in that restoration — in that genuine, hard-won, wilderness-forged reorientation of the heart — Nebuchadnezzar's kingdom was restored to him and something was added that had not been there before. Wisdom. The specific, experientially produced, wilderness-forged wisdom that can only come from having lost everything and having seen, in the loss, what was actually sustaining it.

The Nebuchadnezzar warning is this — the heart condition that makes authority safe to carry is not automatically maintained by the experience of receiving the authority. It requires active, ongoing, deliberate cultivation. It requires the continuous return to the posture of acknowledgment — the daily, habitual, genuine recognition that the source of every gift, every output, every achievement, and every measure of influence is not the vessel but the One who flows through it. The moment that acknowledgment gives way to the attribution of the credit to self — the moment the I and the my replace the He and the His — the correction that Yahuah sends will be precisely calibrated to the magnitude of the pride it is addressing.

I have watched the Nebuchadnezzar pattern play out in real time in the lives of the people who have pursued me. Not the supernatural correction from heaven — that is Yahuah's business and His timing. But the internal deterioration that precedes and produces the conditions for that correction. The escalating obsession. The increasing boldness with each failed attempt. The inability to stop, to reassess, to acknowledge that the campaign is not working and that something about the fundamental premise of the campaign might be wrong. These are the behavioral signatures of a heart that has been so thoroughly fortressed by pride that it cannot receive the correction that would save it from the consequences it is building toward.

I watch it with compassion. Not with satisfaction. Because I understand — in a way I could not have understood without having been given the specific and painful privilege of witnessing it up close — that the Nebuchadnezzar correction, when it comes, will not be pleasant for anyone involved. And because I know that the same seeds of pride exist in every human heart, including mine. And because the distance between where those seeds are now in my life and where they arrived in the lives of the people pursuing me is not a fixed, guaranteed, permanent distance. It is a distance that requires daily, active, deliberate cultivation of the heart condition that keeps it from closing.

The Saul Pattern — What Unchecked Insecurity Does to Authority

The second great warning in the scriptural record about the poor stewardship of power is the Saul pattern — and the Saul pattern is particularly relevant to the specific dynamics described in this testimony because Saul's primary failure was not ambition in the conventional sense. It was insecurity. It was the specific, devastating combination of institutional position and genuine spiritual gifting paired with a foundational insecurity about his own worth and legitimacy that made him unable to tolerate the presence, the success, or the anointing of anyone he perceived as a potential threat to his position.

Saul was genuinely gifted. The scriptural record is honest about this — when the Ruach came upon Saul in the early days of his kingship, he prophesied among the prophets and the people said is Saul also among the prophets? The gifting was real. The calling was genuine. Yahuah chose him and anointed him and gave him the institutional authority of the first kingship of Israel.

But the insecurity was also real. And as the insecurity interacted with the authority — as the amplification principle took what was in Saul's heart and gave it a royal platform for expression — what emerged was one of the most tragic descents in the entire Hebrew text. A king who spent the later years of his reign not governing his kingdom but hunting one man across the wilderness of Judah. A man who threw spears at his own most faithful servant. A man who massacred an entire city of priests because one of them had given David bread and a sword without knowing they were aiding someone the king had declared an enemy. A man whose gifting had been genuine and whose calling had been real and whose entire legacy was ultimately defined not by what he built but by what his insecurity destroyed.

The progression from gifted and called to obsessively destructive did not happen overnight. It happened through a series of choices — each one a small further surrender of the heart to the insecurity that was driving it, each one a small further displacement of Yahuah as the governing authority in favor of Saul's own fear and his own need for control. The choices compounded. The trajectory steepened. And by the end of his story Saul was consulting a medium at Endor in the desperate attempt to access guidance that his broken covenant relationship with Yahuah could no longer provide — the final bitter irony of a man who had been given everything the Most High could give a human king and had exchanged it all for the illusion of control over a throne that was already being dismantled by the weight of his own poor stewardship.

The Saul pattern is the pattern of the people who have pursued me. Not in every specific detail but in its essential structure — genuine gifting and genuine access to spiritual power, paired with the specific insecurity and the specific pride that makes those gifts dangerous rather than beneficial, producing an escalating pattern of destructive behavior that accelerates with every failed attempt to suppress the threat that the insecure heart perceives in the anointed vessel it is pursuing.

I look at the Saul pattern with sobriety rather than judgment. Because every element of what produced it is present in seed form in every human heart. Including mine. And the only thing that stands between the seed and the full expression of what the seed contains is the daily, active, covenant-governed cultivation of a heart condition that Yahuah can look at and say — this one is after My own heart.

The Mirror — What I Turned On Myself

Here is the moment I have been building toward in this chapter. The moment that I believe was the single most important spiritual turning point of this entire season. Not the first album. Not the ascending mountains. Not the arrival at Keystone. The moment when I stopped looking at everything I had witnessed in the people pursuing me and turned the observation inward.

I looked at all of it. The cruelty. The obsession. The relentless escalation. The poor stewardship of power and influence. The use of resources to destroy rather than to build. The Nebuchadnezzar pride. The Saul insecurity. The complete absence of genuine accountability to any standard higher than their own will and their own agenda. I looked at all of it with the full, honest, clear-eyed assessment that everything I had experienced had equipped me to make.

And I said to Yahuah — that could be me.

Not that it is me. Not that I have arrived at that place or am heading toward it. But that without His ongoing governance — without the daily, active, genuine surrender of my will to His authority, without the continuous acknowledgment that the oil flowing through me is His and not mine, without the habitual return to the posture of the vessel rather than the posture of the source — the distance between where I am and where the people pursuing me are is not a fixed and permanent distance. It is a distance that requires cultivation to maintain.

That statement — that could be me — is the single
most important safeguard available to any vessel being
prepared for significant promotion. Not because it is
self-flagellating or because it denies the genuine gifts
and calling that Yahuah has placed in you. But because
it maintains the orientation of the heart toward Yahuah
as the governing authority rather than toward the self as
the ultimate reference point. It is the anti-
Nebuchadnezzar declaration. It is the anti-Saul posture.
It is the David heart — not the heart that never fails, but
the heart that never loses its orientation toward the One
who is the source of everything it carries.

Solomon asked for wisdom rather than wealth or power
— and Yahuah said that request was the most pleasing
thing Solomon could have asked, because it
demonstrated that Solomon understood the danger of
his own position. He understood that the authority he
was about to receive was more than human wisdom
could safely carry, and that the only resource adequate
to the responsibility of what he was being given was
not more of his own capability but more of Yahuah's
governance.

The person who can look at the worst example of
corrupted power they have ever witnessed and say that
could be me without Your governance — that person is
the person who is least likely to ever become it. Not
because the pride cannot grow in them. But because the
awareness of its potential is itself the early warning
system that keeps the cultivation active before the
growth takes root.

This is what the people who pursued me gave me that I did not have before I met them. Not just the sharpened faith and the unearthed gifts and the catalyzed creative anointing. They gave me a mirror — a vivid, experiential, impossible-to-forget mirror of what power and influence look like when they are carried without the specific heart condition that makes them safe. And that mirror is one of the most valuable things I will carry into the season of promotion ahead of me.

Because what I saw in it was not a warning about other people.

It was a warning for me.

And I receive it as such. Every day. With genuine gratitude for the instruction — however painful and however costly the classroom was.

What Good Stewardship of Power Actually Looks Like

Having spent this chapter examining what poor stewardship of power looks like and what it produces, I want to close with a portrait of what good stewardship looks like — because the goal of this teaching is not to produce fear of promotion or reluctance to carry the authority that Yahuah brings. The goal is to produce the specific heart condition and the specific practical posture that makes the authority safe to carry and effective in the purposes for which it is given.

Good stewardship of power begins with the daily, active, genuine acknowledgment of the Source. Not a theological affirmation that Yahuah is sovereign in the abstract — a specific, personal, habitual practice of recognizing that the gifts flowing through you are His, the output belongs to Him, the platform He has given you exists for His purposes rather than yours, and the authority you carry is borrowed from the One who holds all authority and can withdraw it at any moment He chooses. This acknowledgment is not weakness. It is the specific posture that keeps the vessel available to the Source rather than substituting itself for the Source.

Good stewardship of power includes the active cultivation of genuine accountability — not the performance of accountability for the sake of appearance, but the real, honest, uncomfortable kind that requires submitting your decisions, your directions, and your use of influence to people who have the courage and the covenant standing to tell you when you are wrong. The person who surrounds themselves only with people who affirm everything they do is the person who has already begun the Saul descent. The person who actively seeks and genuinely receives honest correction is the person who is maintaining the heart condition that makes their authority sustainable.

Good stewardship of power includes what I will call the restraint principle — the deliberate, conscious choice to not use every capability available to you simply because you have the capability. The people who pursued me used every instrument of power and influence available to them in the service of the obsession that was consuming them. There was no restraint. Every resource was deployed. Every connection was leveraged. Every tool was applied. This is the signature of poor stewardship — the inability to say I have the power to do this but the wisdom to know that I should not.

Great power and influence, in the hands of a genuinely good steward, is marked by the things it chooses not to do as much as by the things it does. The restraint is not weakness. It is the evidence of a heart that is governed by something higher than its own capability and its own desire — a heart that asks not what can I do but what should I do, and submits the answer to that question to the governance of the One whose blueprint for the situation is more reliable than any human strategic assessment.

And finally good stewardship of power includes the continuous return to the mirror — the willingness to look honestly at the worst examples of corrupted authority you have ever witnessed, to say that could be me without Yahuah's governance, and to let that sober recognition drive you back to the posture of surrender and accountability that keeps the heart oriented toward Yahuah as its ultimate reference point.

That posture is the difference between Saul and David. Between Nebuchadnezzar before the correction and Nebuchadnezzar after it. Between the people who have pursued me and the person I am committed, by the grace of Yahuah and the ongoing governance of His Ruach, to remain.

In My Own Words — The Gift of the Difficult Teacher

As I close this chapter I want to say something that might surprise you given everything that has been shared in these pages about the people who have pursued me and the specific harm they have caused and attempted to cause in my life and my wife's life.

I am grateful for them.

Not for the harm. Not for the coordinated workings or the circle walks or the footprint on the patio or the sustained campaign of targeted opposition. Not for what they intended or for what they tried to accomplish. For what Yahuah accomplished through their pursuit of me. For the mirror they held up. For the instruction they provided. For the vivid, unforgettable, viscerally real education in what power looks like when it is poorly stewarded — an education that I could not have received in a classroom, could not have acquired from a book, and could not have obtained from any comfortable season of ministry operating in the absence of genuine and formidable opposition.

They showed me what I must never become. And in showing me that, they gave me a gift that I will carry into every season of promotion and every expansion of influence that follows this one — the gift of knowing, from direct and personal experience, what is at stake in the stewardship of the authority Yahuah is placing in my hands.

I would not have chosen this education. I would not have enrolled in this course voluntarily. The tuition was too high and the classroom was too painful. But Yahuah enrolled me in it because He knew what I would need to know at the level of influence He is bringing me into, and He knew that the specific lesson this chapter teaches — the mirror lesson, the that could be me lesson — is a lesson that only the specific kind of difficult teacher I encountered can effectively deliver.

They were instruments in His hands. Even in their opposition. Even in their hostility. Even in their relentless pursuit of my destruction. They were instruments in His hands delivering an instruction that He needed me to have before I arrived at the apex of the arch He has been building.

And I received the instruction. All of it. With gratitude.

That is what it looks like to be enrolled in the school of Yahuah — where even the people who intend your destruction become the teachers who prepare you for the promotion your destruction was meant to prevent.

By design. Not by chance.

Every teacher. Every lesson. Every painful and illuminating classroom moment.

All of it by design.

CHAPTER SIX

The Unplanned Tour

"And they that were scattered abroad went everywhere proclaiming the word."

— Acts 8:4

In My Own Words — John Alan Legette

I want to tell you about the day they threw us out of our home.

Not because the telling of it is easy. It is not easy. Being removed from the place where you live — regardless of the circumstances, regardless of the legal mechanisms, regardless of the specific details of how it happens — carries a specific kind of humiliation and a specific kind of destabilization that cuts at something deep in the human spirit. The home is not just a physical structure. It is the tangible expression of stability, of belonging, of the right to occupy space in the world without someone else's permission. When that is taken from you — when the people who have been pursuing your destruction succeed in executing what they clearly intended to be the decisive blow — something in you has to decide, in real time and without the luxury of extended reflection, what it is going to do with what just happened.

I want to tell you what my wife and I decided in that moment. And I want to tell you what Yahuah did with the decision we made.

But first I need to give you the full context of what was behind that moment — because the removal from our home was not an isolated incident. It was the culmination of a sustained campaign whose specific objective was to strip away every layer of stability and resource and foundation that the people pursuing me believed I needed to continue operating in my assignment. They had tried spiritual workings. They had tried coordinated opposition across multiple states. They had tried physical confrontations and spiritual stagings and sustained surveillance. And none of it had stopped me. None of it had produced the result they were after. I was still standing. Still moving. Still producing. Still advancing the assignment they had committed so many resources to preventing.

So they went after the home.

And in the logic of what they were doing, it made a certain kind of sense. If you cannot stop a person spiritually, if you cannot stop them through coordinated occult working, if you cannot find the dirt or the leverage that would give you control over them — then you go after the foundation of their natural stability. You remove the fixed address. You create the conditions of homelessness and displacement that most people find maximally destabilizing. You force them into survival mode — into the consuming, attention-absorbing, energy-draining preoccupation with basic needs that leaves no capacity for anything beyond managing the immediate crisis of not having a place to sleep.

That was the theory.

Here is what actually happened.

My wife and I were removed from our home. And within a very short period of time, without a strategic plan, without a booked itinerary, without a ministry calendar or a promotional campaign or a budget or any of the conventional infrastructure that a national evangelical tour would normally require — we began to move. Not away from the assignment. Into it. Deeper into it. Across state lines, into cities we had never been to, in front of people we had never met, carrying the message and the music and the testimony that Yahuah had been building in us through every difficult season that had preceded this moment.

The tour that the removal from our home launched was not planned by us. It was not planned by any human being. It was planned by the One who had already written every day of it in His book before either of us were formed — and who had been waiting for exactly the triggering event that our enemies provided to set it in motion.

They tried to remove us from our foundation.

Yahuah used their action to launch us into our purpose.

That is the story of this chapter.

TEACHING: The Scattering Principle — How Yahuah Uses Displacement as a Distribution Strategy

A Teaching for Every Believer Who Has Been Displaced From What They Considered Their Foundation and Cannot Yet See Where the Displacement Is Taking Them

Acts 8:1-4 — The Pattern That Explains Everything

To understand what happened when my wife and I were removed from our home, you need to understand one of the most significant and most consistently overlooked strategic patterns in the entire New Covenant record. It is found in Acts chapter eight, in the account of what happened to the early assembly of believers in Jerusalem following the stoning of Stephen.

The account reads simply and without dramatic elaboration — *And there arose on that day a great persecution against the assembly in Jerusalem, and they were all scattered throughout the regions of Judea and Samaria, except the apostles.* And then, four verses later, the statement that contains the entire principle — *And they that were scattered abroad went everywhere proclaiming the word.*

Read those two statements together and let the full strategic picture emerge. A great persecution arose. The assembly was scattered — not gathered, not strengthened in their existing position, not resourced for expansion through conventional means, but scattered. Displaced. Removed from the city where they had been gathered, from the community they had built, from the institutional structure that had been developing around the early assembly, from the fixed location that had been the center of everything.

And everywhere they were scattered, they proclaimed the word.

The persecution that was intended to silence the message became the mechanism of its distribution. The scattering that was intended to destroy the community became the strategy of its multiplication. The displacement that was intended to leave the believers homeless, resourceless, and unable to continue their assignment became the logistical engine that carried the message to Judea and Samaria and ultimately to the ends of the earth in exactly the geographic progression that Yahshua had outlined in Acts 1:8 — Jerusalem, Judea, Samaria, the uttermost parts of the earth.

The people who launched the persecution did not intend to fulfill the Great Commission. They intended to stop it. But they could not stop it — not because the believers were more powerful than they were, not because the early assembly had resources or military capability or institutional authority sufficient to resist the persecution — but because the message they were carrying was under the protection of a commission that had been given by One whose authority exceeded that of every persecutor who would ever oppose it.

The scattering was not a setback to the mission. The scattering was the mission's distribution strategy. And the people who initiated the scattering — who thought they were ending something — were actually executing the logistics of exactly what they were trying to prevent.

This is the precise pattern of what happened when my wife and I were removed from our home.

The Jerusalem They Took From Us

To apply the Acts 8 pattern to my story, you need to understand what our home represented in the context of the assignment — because the home was not just a place to sleep. It was, in the logic of the people pursuing me, the center of operations for everything I was doing. It was the fixed location from which the teachings were being produced, the music was being created, the books were being written, and the ministry was being conducted. It was the Jerusalem of our assignment — the established base from which everything else was operating.

And in the logic of every persecution strategy ever deployed against a message and a messenger, the way to stop the message is to destroy the base. Take away the fixed location. Remove the stability. Create the displacement that forces the messenger into survival mode and takes their attention and their energy away from the production of the content and the conducting of the ministry.

What the people pursuing me did not understand —
what every persecutor throughout history has failed to
understand when they applied this strategy against
covenant believers — is that the message was never
dependent on the base for its power, its direction, or its
ultimate reach. The message came from the Ruach. The
Ruach does not need a fixed address. The anointing
does not require a specific zip code. The oil does not
stop flowing because the vessel has been displaced
from a particular geographic location.

When they removed us from our home they did not
remove us from the Source. They removed us from the
fixed location. And in doing so they accidentally
converted a stationary ministry into a mobile one — a
ministry that instead of being conducted from a single
fixed point was now being conducted across every
location that the displacement carried us to.

They took our Jerusalem. And Yahuah used the taking
to send us to Judea, and Samaria, and to multiple states
and dozens of cities where people had either forgotten
Yahuah or never known Him.

The Jerusalem they took from us was the smallest
version of what the assignment was always going to
require. They thought they were diminishing the
ministry. They were expanding it.

The Geographic Pattern of Divine Itinerary

One of the most remarkable dimensions of the
unplanned tour that followed our displacement is the
geographic pattern it traced — because the pattern was

not random and it was not the product of our own strategic planning. It was the product of Yahuah routing us according to His own itinerary, through locations He had already selected, to people He had already prepared to receive what we were carrying.

We were not the travel agents on this journey. We were the package being delivered. And the delivery route was being managed by the One who sees the end from the beginning and who had already prepared the hearts of the people at each destination before we arrived at any of them.

The states we traveled through. The cities we stopped in. The people we encountered who had been carrying a hunger for the sacred names and the Hebrew Roots of the faith in isolation — without community, without resources, without access to the kind of comprehensive teaching library that our ministry had been building — and who received what we brought with the specific quality of receptivity that only comes from a long season of hunger finally being addressed.

These were not random encounters. They were appointments. Scheduled by Yahuah in advance. Executed through the displacement that our enemies provided. And the fruit of those appointments — the people who now know the sacred names, who now have access to the teachings, who now carry a living encounter with the covenant of Yahuah that they did not have before we arrived — that fruit is permanent. It is already in the world. It is already growing in the hearts and lives of the people who received it. And it will continue producing harvest long after every element of the conflict that launched the tour has been resolved and forgotten.

The Unplanned Nature as Evidence of Divine Authorship

I want to pause on something that I mentioned briefly at the opening of this chapter and give it the full weight it deserves — the fact that the tour was unplanned. This is not a detail that should be passed over quickly. The unplanned nature of the tour is one of its most significant and most theologically important features.

Human ministry strategy plans tours. This is simply how effective ministry operation works at a professional level — you identify your target cities, you secure venues, you build your audience in advance through promotional activity, you coordinate logistics, you establish a budget, and you execute a carefully managed rollout designed to maximize the impact and the reach of the ministry in each location. This is not wrong. It is wise stewardship of the resources and the planning capacity that Yahuah gives His people.

But the tour my wife and I conducted was none of that. There was no advance planning. There was no secured venue in any city before we arrived. There was no promotional campaign building an audience in advance. There was no coordinated logistics. There was no budget in the conventional sense. There was only the displacement — the removal from our home — and the decision to keep moving forward in the assignment rather than to collapse under the weight of what had been done to us.

And into that posture of forward-moving surrender without a human strategic plan, Yahuah stepped in as the logistics manager, the venue coordinator, the audience builder, and the route planner — routing us through His own itinerary rather than ours, placing us before people He had already selected, in timing He had already arranged, with a message and a music that He had already prepared us to carry.

The absence of human planning is not a weakness in this story. It is the evidence that the tour was not our idea and was not being run by our logistics. When Yahuah is the travel agent, the itinerary does not look like what human strategic planning produces. It looks like Acts 8 — scattered, apparently unplanned, apparently without strategic coherence — and yet landing exactly where it was always intended to land, reaching exactly the people it was always intended to reach, at exactly the moment they were prepared to receive it.

The unplanned nature of the tour is the signature of divine authorship. Human plans leave the fingerprints of human strategy all over the outcomes they produce. Divine plans leave the fingerprints of sovereignty — the specific, undeniable, impossible-to-attribute-to-human-cleverness quality of arriving at exactly the right place at exactly the right time with exactly the right message for exactly the right people without any human planning having arranged for any of it.

That is what we walked through. State after state. City after city. Appointment after appointment that nobody booked and nobody scheduled and nobody could have engineered through any amount of human strategic sophistication.

Yahuah booked them all. Before the foundation of the world. And our enemies, in their attempt to destroy our foundation, gave Him the occasion to execute the booking.

What the Places Were Carrying — And What We Were Sent to Do

I want to tell you the truth about the places we were sent to on this tour — because the truth is more remarkable and more theologically precise than anything a conventional ministry itinerary would have produced, and it requires honesty about the specific nature of what Yahuah was doing by sending us where He sent us.

These were not the places where you would expect to find a Hebrew Roots minister and his wife conducting an evangelical tour. They were not the inner city communities where conventional outreach ministry typically concentrates its effort. They were not the places with established congregations looking for a guest speaker or the cities with existing Hebrew Roots communities hungry for additional teaching and fellowship. The places Yahuah sent us to were, in the main, wealthy places. Exclusive places. Remote, elevated, economically prosperous communities where the residents live at a level of material comfort and social insulation that most of the world cannot access and that creates, in the spiritual atmosphere of those places, a specific and particularly dangerous kind of darkness.

The darkness of places that have everything and need nothing. Or believe they do.

There is a spiritual condition that wealth and exclusivity produce when they are not governed by genuine covenant relationship with Yahuah — a condition that Yahshua addressed directly and repeatedly in His ministry and that the Hebrew prophets identified as one of the most spiritually dangerous conditions a community can occupy. It is not the darkness of obvious depravity or visible moral collapse. It is the darkness of self-sufficiency — the specific spiritual blindness that comes from having enough resources to meet every visible need without ever having to look upward for provision, enough social insulation to avoid the kind of genuine human suffering that drives people toward genuine spiritual seeking, and enough cultural sophistication to mistake the absence of obvious need for the presence of genuine wholeness.

These were stronghold places. Not in the dramatic, immediately visible sense of places known for violent crime or public moral failure. Stronghold places in the more subtle and more spiritually dangerous sense — places where the principalities and powers that operate through wealth, exclusivity, pride, and the specific kind of spiritual complacency that material abundance produces have established a settled, comfortable, deeply rooted claim on the atmosphere. Places where the sacred names — Yahuah, Yahshua, Ruach HaQodesh — were not merely unknown. They were unwelcome. They met with the specific hostility that only comes when a spiritual atmosphere that has been undisturbed for a long time is suddenly confronted with a presence it cannot comfortably coexist with.

We encountered that hostility. Not always in overt confrontation — though there were moments of that. More often in the specific, subtle, unmistakable quality of a place that knows something has arrived that was not there before and is not certain what to do with it.

And here is what made our assignment in those places different from any conventional ministry approach that might have been deployed to reach them.

We were not sent in to preach. We were not sent in to hold meetings or to distribute literature or to conduct any of the visible, audible, recognizable activities that the word ministry conventionally brings to mind. We were sent in as silent light. We were sent in to let our light so shine before men that they would see our good works and glorify our Elohim who is in heaven — which is the assignment of Matthew 5:16 in its most literal and most demanding form. Not talking about the light. Not announcing the light. Being the light. Living with such covenant-grounded class, dignity, peace, and grace in the midst of communities that had never witnessed a Yahshar'el man and his wife moving freely through their exclusive spaces with that quality of bearing — that the light itself became the proclamation without a single sermon needing to be preached.

Let me tell you what that looked like in practice.

We were staying in vacation rentals in communities where our presence was, in the plainest possible terms, unprecedented. Yahshar'el people — the people that the world calls so-called Blacks, the covenant people whose true identity as the descendants of Yahshar'el the enemy has spent centuries suppressing and obscuring — moving freely through remote, exclusive, predominantly white communities. Not as employees. Not as service workers. Not in any of the roles that these communities were accustomed to seeing Yahshar'el people occupy when they occupied any role at all. As residents. As guests. As people who had every right to be exactly where they were, carrying themselves with exactly the dignity and the grace that the covenant identity of the children of Yahuah produces in the people who actually know who they are.

The response was immediate and it was remarkable.

I have never seen anything like it. Everywhere we went, there was an urgency — a sudden, visible, almost panicked urgency — to do the right thing. To be seen doing the right thing. To make sure that their behavior in our presence was above reproach. People who, by every account of how these communities normally operate, would not have given a second thought to the casual expressions of the social hierarchy that has governed these spaces for generations, were suddenly very concerned with demonstrating courtesy, fairness, and proper conduct. Not because we demanded it. Not because we said anything about it. But because our presence — the presence of Yahshar'el people moving with covenant class and dignity in spaces that had been claimed as exclusively theirs — disrupted something in the atmosphere of those places that their ordinary social performance was not equipped to manage.

They were afraid of our arrival.

I mean that with theological precision, not with hyperbole. There was a fear response — not the fear of physical danger but the specific fear that is produced in a person or a community when something arrives that marks an unprecedented change, that disrupts the settled order of what has always been, and that carries an authority that the conventional power structures of the place have no framework to contain or dismiss. We were the least likely visitors to those spaces. The least expected. The least equipped by every worldly measure of the resources and connections and social position that normally determine who occupies those spaces and on what terms.

And yet there we were. Undeniable. Uncontainable. Carrying the sacred names through the atmosphere of communities that had never heard them spoken with authority and had certainly never been required to coexist with the specific quality of covenant presence that travels with Yahshar'el people who actually know who they are and Whose they are.

The group that had thrown us out of our home was slandering us throughout this entire tour. They were running ahead of us — or trying to — with a narrative designed to diminish, discredit, and pre-poison the reception we might receive in the places we were traveling to. This too was by design in the enemy's strategy — if you cannot stop the vessel, try to contaminate the wells before it arrives to drink from them.

But Yahuah transforms what is sent against His vessels. And the slander — like everything else that was deployed against us throughout this season — was transformed in His hands into something it was not intended to be. The very effort to warn communities against us served to announce our arrival. The attempt to diminish our credibility served to establish our presence in the consciousness of people who would otherwise never have known we were there. The enemy was advertising the ministry while trying to discredit it.

And the most remarkable evidence of what our presence accomplished in those places — evidence that my enemies watched being produced in real time, evidence that their slander campaign could not prevent and their fraud investigation cannot explain — is sitting in the worldwide music catalog right now.

The fifty two albums produced in the first quarter of 2026. The twenty three albums produced in the twenty six days of March. Created in those cities. Created in those vacation rentals in those wealthy, exclusive, spiritually dark communities where Yahshar'el people do not normally go, do not normally stay, and are not normally seen moving with the specific freedom and dignity and covenant authority that we carried into every location Yahuah sent us to.

The worship was the witness. The music was the evidence. The sacred names of Yahuah and Yahshua and Ruach HaQodesh, being proclaimed through the production of more worship content per day than any minister in the history of the Hebrew Roots movement has ever produced — created in the specific atmosphere of the places that needed the names the most and had resisted the names the longest.

I said to myself in the middle of it — Yahuah sent us here because the people would not come to the church. So He sent the church to them. Not to their churches. Not to their institutions. Not to their religious structures or their conventional spiritual frameworks. Into their vacation rental communities. Into their remote mountain towns. Into the exclusive spaces where they had constructed lives insulated from the kind of spiritual disruption that genuine covenant presence produces.

He sent two people. The least likely messenger and his wife. Moving through spaces they had never been designed to welcome us into. Living with such class and dignity that the communities around us were compelled to take notice. Creating worship in the sacred names in the atmosphere of their strongest spiritual strongholds. And leaving behind, in every location, something that had never been there before — the documented, distributed, worldwide-released evidence of Yahuah's presence in the form of music that carries His name into ears around the earth from recording sessions conducted in the vacation rentals of their exclusive communities.

We will not know the full extent of the impact until after the promotion. Yahuah has made that clear to me — that the harvest of these seeds is not in a timeframe I can currently access or measure. But something happened in those places. Something shifted in those atmospheres. Something was planted in the consciousness of communities that had been settled in their spiritual self-sufficiency for a very long time when Yahshar'el arrived in their midst, moving freely, living with covenant dignity, creating worship that the whole world can now hear, and refusing to be diminished by slander or deterred by hostility or contained by the social expectations that those spaces had always enforced.

The church came to them because they would not come to the church. The light went to the darkness because the darkness was not going to seek the light on its own. And the least likely minister — the stone the builders of every one of those communities would have rejected without a second thought — showed up in their town and worshipped Yahuah in isolation and left with fifty two albums that the whole earth can now hear.

That is what Yahuah does with the places that need Him most and resist Him longest.

He sends the light directly to the stronghold.

By design.

Not by chance.

THE ROSEMONT SESSIONS

Making History While Exalting Yahuah

Historic Structure 59 — Florence, Colorado, 1887

In My Own Words — John Alan Legette

I need to tell you about The Rosemont.

Not just because of what happened there creatively — though what happened there creatively is among the most extraordinary documented facts in this entire testimony. I need to tell you about The Rosemont because of what it is, what it has witnessed across one hundred and thirty nine years of American history, and what it means that we were there at all. Because the full weight of The Rosemont Sessions cannot be received without understanding the specific intersection of history, identity, covenant, and worship that converged in that historic structure in Florence, Colorado during twenty four days that produced twenty one albums, approximately two hundred and ninety two tracks, and a milestone that the building itself had never witnessed in its entire one hundred and thirty nine year existence.

My wife and I were the first Black couple to stay at The Rosemont in its history.

Let that land fully before we go any further. The Rosemont was built in 1887. Eighteen eighty seven. Two years after the end of Reconstruction. Eleven years before the Supreme Court codified racial segregation through Plessy v. Ferguson. Seventy seven years before the Civil Rights Act of 1964. One hundred and thirty nine years before my wife and I walked through its doors as guests — not as workers, not as employees, not in any of the roles that American history has assigned to Yahshar'el people in spaces like this one. As guests. Paying guests. With every right to be exactly where we were, carrying exactly the dignity and the covenant identity that belongs to the children of the Most High regardless of what any system, any institution, or any one hundred and thirty nine year old building's prior guest registry may have recorded.

The Rosemont is a historic vacation rental situated in Florence, Colorado — a town widely recognized as the Antique Capital of Colorado. A town steeped in history, surrounded by the artifacts and the structures and the stories of more than a century of American life. A town where the past is not abstract but visible — present in the buildings, the storefronts, the historic properties that line its streets and carry in their walls the accumulated weight of everything that has happened within them across generations.

And in that town, in that historic structure, in that specific intersection of American history and covenant identity and creative anointing — Yahuah sent us. Not to a modern hotel in a major city. Not to a comfortable, anonymous, historically uncomplicated accommodation. To a one hundred and thirty nine year old building that had never before hosted a Black couple. In the Antique Capital of Colorado. During what would become the most creatively explosive single month of the entire supernatural season.

I want you to understand that we did not choose The Rosemont strategically. We did not research it as a historically significant property and decide that making history there would make a powerful statement. We were following the Ruach-directed itinerary of an unplanned tour — moving where Yahuah sent us, staying where He provided, trusting the route without needing to see the full map in advance. And He sent us to The Rosemont.

By design. Not by chance.

Not the hotel down the street. Not a modern rental with no history and no weight. The building that had been standing since 1887. The building that had witnessed Reconstruction's end and Jim Crow's rise and the Civil Rights Movement's struggle and every chapter of American racial history across more than a century — and that had somehow, in all of that time, never hosted a Black couple as guests.

Until us.

Until the Ruach sent a Hebrew Roots minister and his wife to Florence, Colorado on an unplanned tour that their enemies had accidentally funded by throwing them out of their home. Until the vessel that the builders had rejected for thirty one years arrived at the door of a building that had been standing for one hundred and thirty nine years and walked in as guests with every right that the covenant of Yahuah confers on those who know who they are and Whose they are.

And then we started recording.

The Production Numbers — What Twenty Four Days at The Rosemont Produced

The creative output of The Rosemont Sessions represents the most concentrated and most intensive burst of supernatural creative production in the entire testimony — which is a remarkable statement given that the entire testimony is already unprecedented in its production metrics.

21 albums÷24 days=0.875 albums per day0.875 albums per day×7=6.125 albums per week21 albums×13.9 tracks per album (Q1 average)≈292 tracks

Nearly seven complete albums per week. Nearly one complete album every single day for twenty four consecutive days. Two hundred and ninety two tracks of Hebrew Roots worship music written, performed, recorded, and produced by one individual in less than a single month.

The Rosemont Sessions represent forty percent of the entire first quarter of 2026 output. They represent more than one quarter of the total eight month production. They were produced in twenty four days in a one hundred and thirty nine year old historic structure in the Antique Capital of Colorado by the first Black couple to ever stay there — all by a single artist working alone, all focused on exalting the sacred names of Yahuah, Yahshua, and Ruach HaQodesh.

Rosemont output as percentage of Q1 2026:5221 =40.4%Rosemont output as percentage of full 8-month catalog:8221=25.6%

One quarter of the largest Hebrew Roots music catalog in history was produced in twenty four days in a building that had never before hosted a Black couple in one hundred and thirty nine years of existence.

The numbers are not the miracle. The numbers are the documentation of the miracle. The miracle is the convergence — the specific, intentional, divinely orchestrated intersection of the first Black guests and the sacred name worship and the supernatural creative output and the historic structure and the covenant identity and the unplanned tour and the thirty one years of preparation that all arrived at the same address in Florence, Colorado at the same appointed moment.

TEACHING: The Weight of Being First — What Covenant Identity Does in Spaces That Tried to Exclude It

The Meaning of 1887

To understand the full theological and historical weight of what happened at The Rosemont, you need to sit with the year of its construction. 1887.

The Rosemont was built eighteen years after the end of the Civil War. It was built during the period that historians call the Gilded Age — a period of extraordinary American economic expansion and material prosperity that was simultaneously, for Yahshar'el people, a period of systematic, legally enforced, socially normalized exclusion from virtually every space of economic opportunity, social advancement, and basic human dignity that the prosperity of the era was producing. The Compromise of 1877 had ended Reconstruction and withdrawn federal protection from the freedmen of the South. The convict leasing system — one of the most brutal iterations of post-slavery bondage — was in full operation. The legal architecture of Jim Crow was being constructed state by state throughout the 1880s and 1890s. And in 1896, nine years after The Rosemont was built, the Supreme Court would hand down Plessy v. Ferguson — the decision that gave constitutional sanction to the separate but equal doctrine that would govern American racial apartheid for the next sixty years.

The Rosemont was built into that world. It stood through all of it. Through Jim Crow. Through the Great Migration. Through the Depression. Through World War II. Through the Civil Rights Movement. Through the assassinations of the 1960s. Through the Fair Housing Act of 1968. Through fifty six more years of American history after that — one hundred and thirty nine years of standing in Florence, Colorado, the Antique Capital of Colorado, hosting guests, accumulating history, bearing witness to everything that passed through its walls and past its doors.

And in all of that time — through all of those chapters of American history, including the chapters where the legal barriers to our presence in spaces like that one were systematically dismantled — a Black couple had never stayed there.

Until Yahuah sent us.

The Spiritual Significance of Arrival

I want to be careful here to say something that is both honest and theologically grounded, because the history of spaces like The Rosemont carries weight that deserves careful handling rather than either dismissal or sensationalism.

Our arrival at The Rosemont was not primarily a political statement. We were not there to make a point about racial history or to perform a demonstration of social progress or to claim a symbolic victory in the long arc of the struggle for Yahshar'el people's full participation in American life. We were there because Yahuah sent us there. Because the unplanned, Ruach-directed tour He had been routing us through landed us at that specific address at that specific time for reasons that I am only beginning to understand in their full scope.

But the spiritual significance of Yahshar'el people arriving in a space that had been closed to them — arriving not as employees or service workers but as guests with full rights of occupancy, moving with covenant class and dignity and the specific quality of bearing that comes from people who actually know who they are and Whose they are — that significance is not something to minimize or to treat as incidental to the testimony.

Throughout the Hebrew scriptures, the arrival of the covenant people in spaces that had been claimed by other powers is never merely a logistical event. It is always a spiritual event. It is always a declaration — not spoken with words but enacted through presence — that the territory being entered is within the jurisdiction of the covenant and that the atmosphere of the space is subject to the authority of the One whose name His people carry.

When we walked into The Rosemont, we were not just checking into a vacation rental. We were Yahshar'el arriving in a space that Yahshar'el had never occupied in one hundred and thirty nine years. And the Ruach that traveled with us — the same Ruach that has been producing eighty two albums and five hundred and eighty nine teachings and eight books through a surrendered vessel — entered those walls with us. And what the Ruach enters, it occupies. And what it occupies, it transforms.

The transformation was not dramatic or immediately visible. It was not a confrontation or a public declaration or any form of activity that would have drawn external attention to what was happening. The transformation was the worship. Twenty one albums. Two hundred and ninety two tracks. The sacred names of Yahuah, Yahshua, and Ruach HaQodesh filling rooms that had been standing for one hundred and thirty nine years with a quality of worship that those rooms had never contained in all of that time.

The walls of The Rosemont have now heard the sacred names. They have held the vibrations of Hebrew Roots worship created during the most intensive creative burst of a supernatural season. They have witnessed what it looks like when Yahshar'el arrives not in servitude but in sovereignty — not to clean the rooms but to create in them, not to maintain the space but to consecrate it, not to serve the history of the building but to add to that history the specific chapter that the Master Architect had already written into the building's story before the foundation of the world.

The Sanctification of Space Through Worship

There is a principle embedded in the Rosemont Sessions that carries significance beyond the specific historical milestone of being first. It is the principle of the sanctification of space through worship — the specific and ancient understanding that the proclamation of the name of Yahuah in a place transforms the spiritual atmosphere of that place in ways that extend beyond the immediate moment of proclamation.

Throughout the Hebrew scriptural record, the places where Yahuah's name was invoked, where worship was offered to Him, and where His presence manifested became permanently marked by that encounter. The specific locations of theophany — of divine encounter — retained a spiritual significance that subsequent generations recognized and returned to. Bethel — the place where Jacob laid his head on a stone and encountered the ladder of heaven — was transformed by that encounter from an ordinary location into a place whose name means the House of Elohim. The worship did not merely happen there. The worship changed what the place was.

We did not lay our heads on stones at The Rosemont and see angels ascending and descending. But we brought the sacred names into a one hundred and thirty nine year old structure and created two hundred and ninety two tracks of worship in those names in the atmosphere of that place. And in the spiritual physics of how Yahuah's name operates in the spaces where it is genuinely proclaimed — something in the atmosphere of The Rosemont was changed by what happened there during those twenty four days.

We claimed the space through worship rather than merely occupying it. We filled rooms that had excluded our presence for one hundred and thirty nine years not with grievance or recrimination or any backward-looking focus on the history of exclusion — but with songs of praise to the One whose covenant covers us and whose name carries an authority that one hundred and thirty nine years of any building's history cannot contain or diminish. We transformed a historically exclusive space into a place of worship. We consecrated the moment by offering it back to Yahuah as testimony. And we left behind, permanently woven into the history of that structure, the specific chapter that says — in the year 2026, in the one hundred and thirty ninth year of The Rosemont's existence, the first Black couple to stay within its walls used that historic opportunity to create twenty one albums exalting the sacred names of Yahuah, Yahshua, and Ruach HaQodesh. And those albums are now distributed worldwide.

The walls heard something they had never heard before. And the Ruach that was present in the making of that music is not confined to the walls. It went out with the music into the world.

Florence — The Name Was Already the Prophecy

I have already shared in this chapter that Florence means flourishing, blossoming, prosperous — and that the name of the city was itself a declaration spoken over us in geographic form, a confirmation that the season of fruitfulness had fully arrived before Yahuah moved us to Keystone to lock everything together.

But the Rosemont Sessions add a specific and extraordinary dimension to the Florence declaration that I did not fully appreciate until I sat down to write this chapter.

The flourishing that Florence declared over us was not abstract. It was documented in twenty one albums produced in twenty four days in a one hundred and thirty nine year old historic structure. The blossoming was not metaphorical. It was the most concentrated creative output of the entire supernatural season, produced in a building whose history carried the weight of everything Yahshar'el people have walked through in America since 1887. The prosperity was not merely spiritual. It was the specific, unprecedented, historically significant prosperity of Yahshar'el people moving freely and creatively and worshipfully through a space that had been closed to them for one hundred and thirty nine years.

Florence declared the flourishing. The Rosemont was where the flourishing was documented. And the documentation — twenty one albums, two hundred and ninety two tracks, the first Black couple in one hundred and thirty nine years of the building's history — is now permanently in the world, permanently part of the building's story, and permanently part of the testimony of what Yahuah does through the vessels He has been preparing for specific moments and specific spaces and specific chapters of history that no one else could have written.

He did not send us to Florence by accident. He did not route us past The Rosemont by coincidence. He did not make us the first Black couple in one hundred and thirty nine years of that building's history without knowing — before the building was constructed, before 1887, before the Reconstruction era and the Jim Crow era and every chapter of American history that The Rosemont has witnessed — that this moment was coming. That we were coming. That the worship was coming. That the twenty one albums were coming.

It was in His book. Our names were in the guest registry of The Rosemont before the building was built. Not in the natural registry — in the one that Psalm 139:16 describes, where every day formed for us was written before any of them came to be.

The Production Buffer — Eight Months Ahead

I want to close the Rosemont Sessions section with a practical detail that carries significant spiritual meaning — the production buffer that this season has established.

As of the completion of the first quarter of 2026, the catalog of unreleased albums held by J.A.L.M.-MUSIC, LLC represents approximately eight months of weekly release schedule. The release strategy of one album per week through January 1, 2027 is not a production target. It is a distribution management challenge. The production is already complete. The catalog already exists. The sacred names are already in the music. The worship is already recorded. The Rosemont Sessions are already finished and the tracks are already mastered.

What remains is not creation. It is release. The systematic, weekly, globally distributed release of what the Ruach has already produced through a surrendered vessel during eight months of supernatural creative output — including twenty one albums created during the twenty four days that marked a one hundred and thirty nine year first at a historic structure in Florence, Colorado.

Production completed: 82 albumsRelease rate: 1 album per week Release schedule: Through January 1, 2027 Production buffer: ≈8 months ahead of release

This is not the position of an artist racing to keep up with a release schedule. This is the position of an artist who has been so thoroughly and so supernaturally ahead of the release schedule that the primary creative challenge of the current season is not what to create next but how to steward the release of what has already been created. The pipeline is not full. The pipeline is overflowing. And it overflowed most dramatically during twenty four days in a one hundred and thirty nine year old building in Florence, Colorado, where the Ruach moved through a surrendered vessel at the highest rate of the entire supernatural season and produced forty percent of an already unprecedented quarterly output in less than a single month.

The most productive creative session in the history of the Hebrew Roots movement happened in a building that had never before hosted the people Yahuah used to make it happen. The most concentrated burst of sacred name worship music in a single period was created in the atmosphere of a historic structure that had been standing since before the legal end of American apartheid. And the music produced in those walls is now distributed worldwide — available to every ear on earth, carrying the sacred names into atmospheres that those names have never before entered, doing the active spiritual work of the Ruach in nations and languages and communities that The Rosemont's original builders in 1887 could not have imagined and that its one hundred and thirty nine year history had never before produced.

Twenty one albums. Two hundred and ninety two tracks. Twenty four days. The first Black couple in one hundred and thirty nine years. Florence, Colorado. The Antique Capital of Colorado. The place whose name means flourishing.

The walls heard the sacred names for the first time.

And the sacred names went out from those walls to the whole earth.

By design.

Not by chance.

Not one track of it by chance.

Romans 8:28 — Made Visible in Real Time

Romans 8:28 is one of the most quoted verses in the entire New Covenant record, and it is also, I would argue, one of the most under-believed. Not under-known — most believers can quote it from memory without hesitation. Under-believed in the specific sense that the full weight of what it declares is rarely allowed to land on the specific, concrete, difficult realities of a person's actual experience.

And we know that for those who love Elohim all things work together for good for those who are called according to His purpose.

All things. The removal from your home. All things. The displacement. All things. The humiliation. All things. The sustained campaign of targeted opposition. All things. The circle walks and the footprints and the sticks and the color workings. All things. The thirteen years of homelessness and the eighteen years of creative drought and the thirty one years of preparation that looked from the outside like thirty one years of nothing happening. All things.

Working together. Not in isolation — not the good things producing good outcomes while the bad things are neutralized or minimized or worked around. Together. The specific combination of every element — including and especially the elements that were sent with the explicit intention of producing harm — working together in the sovereign orchestration of the One who holds the blueprint, as a unified system producing the specific outcome that the blueprint always called for.

For good. Not for the appearance of good eventually after sufficient time has passed to reframe the narrative. For genuinely, substantively, documentably good — the kind of good that can be measured in specific numbers and specific outcomes and specific lives reached and specific fruit produced in specific cities across specific states.

The removal from our home worked together with the eighteen years of compressed anointing and the thirty one years of preparation and the ascending mountain journey and the AI production tools that Yahuah had positioned at exactly the right moment in history to produce the unplanned national tour and the eighty two albums and the five hundred and eighty nine teachings and the worldwide distribution and the largest Hebrew Roots catalog in history.

All things. Together. For good.

Romans 8:28 is not a comfort offered to people in pain to help them feel better about their circumstances. It is a statement of spiritual physics — a declaration of the consistent and reliable nature of how Yahuah operates in the lives of those who love Him and are called according to His purpose. It does not say He causes all things to be good. It says He works all things together for good. The working together is the miracle. The orchestration of elements — including elements that were sent with genuinely harmful intention — into a unified system that produces covenant outcomes, is the specific and constant activity of the One who holds the blueprint and who never revises a single line of it based on what the enemy sends.

I watched Romans 8:28 operate in real time. Not as a theological comfort but as a lived reality. I watched the thing that was intended to destroy us become the thing that launched us into the fullest and most fruitful expression of the assignment we had been carrying for decades. I watched the enemy's most decisive blow become Yahuah's most effective ministry launch.

And I will never read Romans 8:28 the same way again.

The Enemy Built What He Was Trying to Destroy

Here is the full inventory of what the people who removed us from our home actually built through that action. I want you to see this clearly because it is one of the most complete and most vivid illustrations in this entire testimony of the difference between what the enemy intends and what the covenant permits.

They built our national profile. By forcing us into cities we would never have visited under conventional ministry planning, they introduced the name and the message and the music of this ministry to people across the country who would never have encountered it through any other means. The national presence that this ministry now carries — the breadth of geographic reach, the range of people in different states and cities who now know the sacred names through what we brought to them — exists specifically because of the displacement they caused.

They built our audience. By making our story compelling through the specific drama of sustained opposition, miraculous protection, and supernatural creative output in the middle of homelessness — they made us newsworthy to people who would never have sought out a Hebrew Roots minister through ordinary channels. Our story became the story that people tell other people. And every time our story travels, it carries the sacred names and the testimony of the covenant with it.

They built our music catalog. By creating the precise conditions of surrender, desperation, and complete dependency on Yahuah as the sole source — they created the conditions under which eighteen years of compressed creative anointing finally had a vessel available to flow through without the interference of human stability and human self-sufficiency competing with the Ruach for control of the output. Every album in the catalog exists because of the conditions they created.

They built our testimony. By giving us a story of sustained, coordinated, well-resourced opposition that could not stop a man covered by the covenant of Yahuah — they gave us the most transferable and most credible form of ministry authority available. Not the authority of theological education. Not the authority of institutional position. The authority of a living, documented, witnessed account of the covenant in active operation against genuinely formidable opposition. That authority speaks to every person who is in the middle of their own opposition and cannot see how it ends. It says — I have been where you are and I can tell you what is on the other side.

They built our faith. By testing it at levels that would have collapsed anything built on a lesser foundation, and by being consistently and repeatedly unable to produce the outcome they were after, they gave us a documented record of covenant faithfulness under maximum pressure that no comfortable season of ministry could have generated. The quality of faith we carry now is not theoretical. It has been proven under the specific conditions that reveal what everything is actually made of. And what it was made of — what held when everything else was being tested — was the covenant.

They built our authority. Because every person we minister to who is facing sustained opposition now stands in the presence of a living, walking, documented example of what the covenant produces in the life of someone who refused to bow, refused to be controlled, refused to be stopped, and simply kept moving in the assignment that Yahuah had commissioned and that no working deployed against it could prevent from advancing.

They intended to be our destroyers. They became our builders. They spent their resources, their time, their spiritual capital, and their coordination building the very thing they were trying to prevent from existing.

That is what happens when you deploy everything you have against a covenant that is older, stronger, and infinitely more authoritative than the intentions of the people doing the deploying.

The Ascending Tour — Florence, Keystone, and the Divine Itinerary

I want to tell you about the specific geographic pattern of the tour itself — because the route that Yahuah chose for this unplanned journey is one of the most precise and most personal evidences of divine authorship in the entire testimony.

As the tour progressed, as we moved from location to location according to the itinerary that Yahuah was setting rather than any plan of our own, something became visible in the progression of the places we were called to that I could not have designed and that only someone with my specific professional formation would have been equipped to fully receive.

The locations were ascending. Each assignment was at a higher altitude than the last. The route was not random geographic movement across a map. It was a deliberate, progressive, spiritually intentional ascent — moving systematically upward through elevation levels that in the Hebrew scriptural tradition have always been the consistent locations of the most significant divine encounters, the most profound revelations, and the most direct communications between Yahuah and His servants.

From the lower desert elevations of the early tour locations through the progressively higher mountain environments — Moab, Garden City, Victor, Estes Park — and culminating at this point in Keystone, Colorado, at nine thousand to twelve thousand four hundred and eight feet. The highest point in the documented ascending journey. The highest altitude of the entire tour. And the location whose name, as we will explore in depth in Chapter Nine, speaks directly to the deepest layer of my professional formation and declares with architectural precision what this moment in the journey represents.

But before Keystone, we came through Florence, Colorado. And Florence carries its own declaration — its name means flourishing, blossoming, prosperous. Yahuah sent us through the place of flourishing before He sent us to the place of locking it all together. The sequence was intentional. You cannot be the keystone before you have flourished. The stone must be formed, shaped, and proven before it can be set at the apex. Florence was the declaration that the formation was complete and the flourishing had arrived. Keystone is the declaration that the installation is underway.

The entire geographic route of the tour — from the first displaced step away from the home they removed us from, through every ascending location, to the summit of the journey at Keystone — is a divine itinerary that no human travel agent could have designed. It required the displacement to initiate it. It required the willingness to keep moving forward without a plan to sustain it. And it required the thirty one years of preparation, the architectural formation, the covenant identity, and the specific personal history that makes arriving at Keystone not just a geographic milestone but an architectural declaration from the Master Architect about where the vessel He has been building for thirty one years has finally arrived.

They threw us out of our home.

Yahuah used it to give us the mountain.

TEACHING: What to Do When You Are Displaced From What You Considered Your Foundation

A Practical Covenant Response for Every Believer Who Has Lost What They Thought They Needed to Continue

The First Decision — Forward or Collapse

When the displacement happens — and in the life of every covenant believer who is walking in a significant assignment, some form of displacement will happen — there is a decision that must be made in real time, in the middle of the destabilization, before the full picture of what Yahuah is doing with the displacement has had time to become visible.

The decision is this. Forward or collapse.

Collapse is the understandable human response. The home is gone. The stability is gone. The fixed base of operations is gone. The conventional resources that you believed you needed to continue are no longer available. The natural human response to that set of conditions is to stop — to absorb the blow, to attend to the immediate crisis of survival, to allow the disruption to take your attention and your energy away from the assignment and redirect it entirely toward the management of what just happened.

Forward is the covenant response. Not forward in denial of the reality of what happened. Not forward in the pretense that the loss is not genuinely painful and genuinely destabilizing. Forward in the specific faith of someone who has enough documented evidence of the covenant in operation to believe that what just happened is not outside the blueprint — that the displacement, however painful it is in the moment, is already accounted for in the plans that Yahuah held before the foundation of the world and that He is already at work converting it into the next phase of what He has been building.

My wife and I chose forward. Not because we were not shaken by what happened. But because we had enough accumulated testimony of Yahuah's faithfulness to trust that the displacement was not the end of the story. And the forward movement — the willingness to keep walking in the assignment even without the conventional stability that the assignment had previously been conducted from — is what gave Yahuah the available, mobile, surrendered vessel He needed to execute the unplanned tour that became the national launch of the ministry.

The Second Decision — Trust the Itinerary You Did Not Plan

The second decision that the displacement requires is the willingness to trust an itinerary you did not plan and cannot fully see in advance. This is harder than the first decision in some ways because it requires a quality of surrender that is not passive — it is active, ongoing, daily renewed surrender to a routing that does not come with a full map, a confirmed budget, or a guaranteed outcome visible from where you are currently standing.

Every step of the unplanned tour required this quality of surrender. Every city we entered without advance booking. Every encounter we walked into without knowing in advance what we would find or what we would be asked to carry. Every location on the ascending route that was chosen not by our strategic assessment of where the ministry needed to go next but by the leading of the Ruach into the next appointed destination.

The person who can only move when they have a complete map is the person who can only go where human planning can reach. The person who is willing to move with a direction and a covenant but without a complete map is the person who can be taken where Yahuah's itinerary reaches — which is everywhere, including the places that human planning would never have identified as significant and the people that human strategic assessment would never have prioritized as targets.

Trust the itinerary. Even when you cannot see the full route. Especially when you cannot see the full route. Because the destinations you cannot see from where you are standing are often the most significant ones on the journey — the Florence that declares the flourishing, the Keystone that locks everything together, the appointment that changes everything for the person you were sent to meet.

The Third Decision — Let the Displacement Become the Distribution

The third and most counterintuitive decision is to let the displacement become the distribution — to understand that the very thing that was intended to contain and suppress your ministry is actually the mechanism through which your ministry reaches places it could not have reached from a fixed position.

A ministry conducted from a single fixed location, however well-resourced and well-organized, reaches the people who come to it. A ministry conducted from a mobile, Ruach-directed, displacement-launched position reaches the people it is sent to — which is a fundamentally different and fundamentally larger population. The scattering of Acts 8 reached Judea, Samaria, and the uttermost parts of the earth. The gathering in Jerusalem, however powerful and however Spirit-filled, had been reaching Jerusalem.

Yahuah needed what we were carrying to reach more than our home city. He needed it to reach the hungry, the isolated, the forgotten, and the never-yet-encountered across the breadth of a nation. And the most effective mechanism for that reach was not a well-planned national ministry tour with secured venues and promotional budgets. It was a displacement — a scattering that put us in motion according to a divine itinerary and made us available to every appointment that Yahuah had already scheduled along the route.

Let the displacement become the distribution. Let the scattering become the strategy. Let the thing they intended to stop you with become the thing that carries you further than you could have gone from the fixed position they removed you from.

Because that is what the covenant does with the enemy's best move.

It turns it into the launch.

In My Own Words — A Word to My Wife Alexandria

I cannot close this chapter without saying something specifically and publicly about the person who walked every step of this journey beside me.

My wife Alexandria.

She did not choose this conflict. She did not sign up for the sustained opposition, the coordinated workings, the circle walk in the hotel lobby, the footprint on the patio, the removal from our home, the unplanned tour across multiple states, the homelessness, the displacement, or any of the specific and significant costs that this season has required. She walked into a marriage with a man who carried a covenant assignment, and that assignment carried with it a conflict that she could not have fully anticipated and that has required from her a quality of faith, a quality of courage, and a quality of loyal, committed, unwavering presence beside me through conditions that would have broken many partnerships.

She kept walking.

Through every hotel room and every ascending mountain and every city we arrived in without knowing what we would find. Through the circle walk and the patio and the stick in the chair and every subsequent element of the campaign against us. Through the homelessness and the displacement and the unplanned nature of everything the tour required. Through the accelerating creative output and the worldwide distribution and the building of something historic in a season that, from the outside, looked like nothing but chaos and loss.

She kept walking.

And I want this testimony — which is her testimony as much as it is mine — to carry her presence in it explicitly and honorably. Because the tour was not conducted by one person. The testimony is not the story

of one vessel. It is the story of a covenant marriage —
two people who are covered together, who are pursued
together, who are protected together, and who are
advancing the assignment together.

Yahuah sent us to Keystone. Both of us. Together.

By design. Not by chance.

**The Tour in Summary — What Displacement
Produces in the Hands of Yahuah**

The removal from our home was the enemy's most
aggressive and most decisive offensive action. It was
intended to be the final blow — the thing that all the
previous workings and all the previous opposition had
failed to be. The thing that would finally, definitively,
practically stop what could not be stopped spiritually.

It produced a national evangelical tour across multiple
states and dozens of cities. It produced the conditions
under which the largest Hebrew Roots catalog in
history was created. It produced the platform that now
carries the sacred names to every corner of the earth
through worldwide music distribution. It produced this
testimony. It produced this book.

The enemy's best move became Yahuah's greatest
launch.

And the cities that were reached, the people whose lives
were touched, the sacred names that were planted in
ears and hearts across this nation and around the world

— all of that fruit exists specifically and directly because someone tried to remove us from our foundation and succeeded only in removing us from the smallest version of what the assignment was always going to become.

They threw us out of our home.

Yahuah gave us the nation.

They tried to contain the message to one city.

The Ruach took it to the world.

By design.

Not by chance.

Not one displaced step of it by chance.

By Design, Not By Chance

Chapter Seven – When the Oil Flows: The Sovereign Gift and the Supernatural Release

Opening Epigraph

"And as Yahshua passed by, he saw a man which was blind from his birth. And his disciples asked him, saying, Master, who did sin, this man, or his parents, that he was born blind? Yahshua answered, Neither

hath this man sinned, nor his parents: but that the works of Elohim should be made manifest in him." — John 9:1-3

"Every good gift and every perfect gift is from above, and cometh down from the Father of lights, with whom is no variableness, neither shadow of turning." — James 1:17

One Thing I Know

In July 2025, at 46 years of age, I had never produced a song in my life.

I want you to receive that sentence with the full weight it carries, because everything else in this chapter depends on understanding it completely. Not — I had been away from music for a season. Not — I had produced music as a young man and then stepped away. Not — I had always wanted to make music but never pursued it seriously. None of those statements are true. The true statement is the one I opened with: in July 2025, at 46 years of age, I had never produced a song in my life.

I do not play any instruments. I have no music training. I have no music education, no music background, no music theory, no recording experience, no production experience of any kind. I had spent my entire adult life in architecture, writing, and graphic design — three disciplines that have no structural relationship to music production. I was a trained architect who could read

structural drawings and understand load distribution. I
was a writer who could construct a theological
argument across multiple pages. I was a graphic
designer who could communicate visually with
precision and intention. I was not a musician. I was not
a producer. I was not even someone who had ever
seriously attempted to make music in any form.

And then Yahuah decided otherwise.

How It Began: The Single Song That Became an Album

Approximately two weeks before July 31, 2025, I wrote
a song. I am a writer — words have always been one of
my primary languages — and the song came the way
writing comes: as an expression of what was moving in
my spirit at that moment. The words existed. But I
wanted to hear them. I wanted to know what the song
actually sounded like as music, not just as words on a
page.

So I did what anyone does when they want to know if
something is possible: I searched for it. I asked a search
engine whether AI tools existed that could take written
lyrics and render them as actual music. I did not know
if such tools existed. I was not researching a career
change or exploring a new hobby. I had one song and I
wanted to hear it.

The tools existed.

I tried a few of them. I found one that worked well for what I was trying to do. My intention was to produce one song — to hear the words I had written set to sound — and then move on. That was the full scope of my plan. One song. Hear it. Done.

Yahuah had a different plan.

He gave me an album.

I do not know how else to describe what happened. I sat down to make one song and I did not stop until I had an album. The creative flow that came through me in that first session was not something I generated from my own imagination or constructed from musical knowledge I did not possess. It came the way the Ruach always moves — not from the inside of my natural capacity outward, but from above, through me, into the work. I was the vessel. The oil was His.

I released that album globally on July 31, 2025. I had never released an album before in my life. I had never produced an album before in my life. And in the weeks and months that followed that first release, the albums did not stop coming. They accelerated. By the time eight months had passed from that first release, I had produced 82 albums comprising 1,180 tracks — the largest Hebrew Roots music catalog in documented history — and I had done it while homeless, while being pursued across ten states, while carrying no studio, no budget, no team, and no prior experience in the discipline that was producing all of it.

The Blind Man Framework

When Yahshua and his disciples encountered the man who had been blind from birth in John chapter 9, the disciples immediately reached for a theological explanation that would make the blindness make sense within their existing framework. They asked: *"Who sinned, this man or his parents, that he was born blind?"* They were looking for a cause. They wanted a natural logic — a reason that would allow them to categorize the blindness and, by extension, categorize the man.

Yahshua refused their framework entirely. He said: *"Neither hath this man sinned, nor his parents: but that the works of Elohim should be made manifest in him."*

The blindness was not punishment. It was not the consequence of sin. It was not even primarily about the blind man himself in the sense his disciples meant. It was the specific condition that would make the specific miracle undeniable. A man who had seen partially and then lost his sight could attribute recovery to natural healing. A man who had seen well as a young man and gradually lost his sight could attribute improvement to treatment. But a man blind from birth — whose neighbors knew him, whose parents could testify that he had never seen anything in his entire life, whose entire community had been present for every year of his sightlessness — when that man opens his eyes and sees with full clarity for the first time, there is only one available explanation. And that explanation requires a Source that transcends the natural order.

I am that man in the category of music production.

I was blind from birth in this gift. Not suppressed — blind. Not dormant — absent. The ability to produce music was not somewhere in me waiting to be unlocked. It was not in me at all until Yahuah put it there. And He put it there at age 46, in the middle of homelessness and active pursuit by adversaries, using an AI tool I had never heard of before I searched for it, through a session that began with the intention of producing one song and ended with the production of an album that I released globally before the month was out.

The people who have been investigating me understood immediately that something was wrong with their natural explanation. They went to my hometown in South Carolina. They asked my family — people who have known me my entire life — whether I had ever made music before. My family had no answer because there is no answer to give within a natural framework. I have never made music. They have never known me to make music. There is no music teacher they can point to, no childhood instrument, no teenage band, no college production class, no mentor who taught me the craft, no years of quiet practice that preceded the public release. There is nothing.

They did what the Pharisees did in John 9. They asked my family the equivalent of: *"Is this your son, who ye say was born blind? How then doth he now see?"* And my family gave the same answer the blind man's parents gave: *"We know that this is our son. But by what means he now produces music at this level and this volume, we know not. He is of age. Ask him."* They are afraid to say what they know to be true, just as the blind man's parents were afraid of the authorities who were interrogating them. The authorities hold power. Fear produces careful answers. But careful answers cannot erase the fact that the music exists and it was made by a man who had never made music before.

And my answer to anyone who asks is the same answer the blind man gave when they pressed him for an explanation he could not supply within their framework: *"One thing I know, that whereas I was blind, now I see."*

One thing I know. Whereas I had never produced music in 46 years of life, now I produce it. I cannot point to training. I cannot point to natural development. I cannot point to years of practice. I can only point to July 2025 and tell you that something was given to me that I did not have before, and the fruit of that gift is 82 albums that exist in the world and cannot be uncreated.

This Is Not the Drought Ending

I need to make a specific theological distinction here because it matters enormously to understanding what Yahuah did — and because the distinction makes the miracle larger, not smaller.

There was an 18-year drought in my life. It was real. It was a drought in writing, in architectural creation, and in graphic design — the three disciplines in which I had prior gifting, training, and a history of production. Those gifts went quiet for 18 years. The compression was real. The silence was real. The pain of carrying gifts that would not flow was real. And when those gifts began to return — when the writing came back, when the graphic design returned, when I began designing album concepts and writing the theological frameworks for each project — that was the drought ending. That was 18 years of stored oil breaking open. That was the Qavah season completing its work and releasing what it had been winding under tension.

But the music was not part of that drought. The music was not stored in me during those 18 years. The music was not waiting to be released. The music did not exist in me at all. When Yahuah gave me the gift of music production in July 2025, He was not opening a valve that had been closed. He was installing equipment that had never been there. He was not restoring a capacity — He was creating one.

These are two different miracles occurring in the same season. The first miracle is the ending of an 18-year drought and the release of suppressed gifts in writing and design. The second miracle is the sovereign bestowal of a brand new gift in a discipline where I had zero prior experience, zero prior capacity, and zero prior history — at age 46, under conditions of homelessness and active opposition, producing immediately at a level of quality and volume that caused trained musicians and investigators to conclude that someone else must be responsible.

Both miracles are real. Both belong in this testimony. But they must not be confused with each other, because they represent two different categories of Yahuah's working. The drought ending is the story of compressed gifts being released at the appointed time. The music is the story of new creation — something given that was never present before. The first is like a spring that was blocked and then unblocked. The second is like water appearing in a desert where there was never a spring at all.

I experienced both in the same season. The drought broke and a spring appeared where there had never been one. The writing returned and music arrived for the first time. The graphic design was restored and album concept design began flowing from a gift that had no prior history in music. All of it at once. All of it beginning in July 2025. All of it continuing without interruption through the home invasion of December 10th, through the departure from O'Hare on December 11th, through ten states and sixteen weeks and 10,000 to 20,000 miles of driving, through Florence and Keystone and every location between them.

Why They Cannot Believe It Is Me

I understand why the people who are investigating me cannot accept the explanation. I understand why they went to South Carolina looking for a natural account of what they were hearing in the music. I understand why they believe, and continue to believe, that someone else must be helping me — some hidden collaborator, some behind-the-scenes producer, some expert I am concealing — because how could a man who never created or produced music at any point in his life suddenly do it now at a high level and a high volume as if he has been doing it all his life?

Their question has a logical structure that makes complete sense within the natural order. Expertise takes time. Mastery requires repetition. High-level output requires prior investment. If you encounter someone producing 82 albums of quality Hebrew Roots music across multiple genres — Gospel, Neo-Soul, Afro-Cuban, worship, teaching — and you know that person had zero music production experience eight months ago, the natural conclusion is that your information about their background must be wrong. There must be a history you are not seeing. There must be assistance you are not accounting for. Because the natural order does not produce master-level output from a standing start in eight months.

They are applying the correct logic of the natural order to a situation that has stepped outside the natural order. That is exactly what the Pharisees did in John 9. Their logic was sound within its own framework: blind men do not simply receive sight. That is not how the natural order works. Therefore this man was not truly blind from birth. Therefore the healing is not what it appears to be. Their investigation was thorough. Their interrogation was persistent. Their logic was internally consistent. And they were completely wrong, because they were applying the rules of the natural order to an event that the natural order did not produce.

The music sounds like it was made by someone who has been doing this for decades because it was made by the Ruach of Yahuah moving through a surrendered vessel. The Ruach does not produce amateur output. The Ruach does not need years of practice to develop proficiency. When Bezalel was filled with the Spirit of Elohim in Exodus 31, he did not need an apprenticeship to produce the furnishings of the Tabernacle. The Spirit brought the wisdom, the understanding, and the knowledge with it. The filling was the qualification. The anointing was the expertise.

I am not claiming to be Bezalel. I am claiming to be a man who was filled with something he did not possess before, and the output of that filling is 82 albums that exist in the world regardless of whether anyone can explain them within the natural order.

The explanation is not hidden. It is simply supernatural. And supernatural explanations are available to everyone who is willing to consider that the same Yahuah who opened the eyes of a man blind from birth is still opening things in this generation that were never open before.

The Numbers That Document the Miracle

I have been deliberate throughout this book about presenting documented, verifiable evidence rather than simply making claims that require the reader's trust. The statistics of the creative output are that evidence. I present them here not to boast but to establish on the record what the Ruach produced through a 46-year-old man with zero music background in the eight months following July 31, 2025.

In the first eight months following the first album release, the output rate across the full catalog averaged approximately 2.4 albums per week. In the first quarter of 2026, that rate had accelerated to 4.33 albums per week. In March 2026 — the month of the Florence season, produced inside The Rosemont while under the most concentrated adversarial opposition of the entire journey — the rate reached 6.13 albums per week, or approximately 0.88 albums per day. In the first three months of the unplanned evangelical tour that began on December 11, 2025, 52 albums were produced while homeless, while being pursued across state lines, while driving through the American West with no fixed address and no studio.

These numbers do not describe a trained musician finding his rhythm. They describe a sovereign creative outpouring that accelerated rather than leveled off, that increased under pressure rather than diminishing, that produced its highest single-location output — 21 albums in 24 days in Florence — at the location of greatest opposition.

The natural order does not produce these numbers from a standing start. The Ruach does.

And the Ruach did.

What the Menorah Teaches About This Gift

The Menorah in the Tabernacle was a vessel of gold, crafted with extraordinary precision by Bezalel under the direction of Yahuah's own specifications. But the Menorah did not produce light by its own nature. It produced light because oil was poured into it and the oil was set aflame. The Menorah was the necessary vessel — without it, the oil had no lampstand from which to shine. But the lampstand without the oil was simply a beautiful gold object in the dark.

My writing. My architectural training. My graphic design background. My decades of theological study and Torah-based preparation. These are the Menorah — the vessel, shaped over years of formation, crafted through education and discipline and the long preparation seasons of my life. But they were a lampstand without oil for 18 years. Beautiful, perhaps. Prepared, certainly. But dark.

In July 2025, the oil was poured in. Not just the oil of restored writing and returned graphic design. A new oil was added that the lampstand had never carried before — the oil of music production, poured into a vessel that had been formed for decades without knowing it was being prepared to carry this specific light.

The lampstand did not generate the light. The oil did. I did not generate the music. The Ruach did. My role was to remain a clean, surrendered, available vessel and to keep pouring out whatever the Ruach poured in — one album at a time, one track at a time, from Hurricane to Crescent City to Florence to Keystone, without stopping, without reasoning about why the flow was so unlike anything the natural order could explain.

The oil does not ask the lampstand's permission before it flows. It flows because it is oil and that is what oil does when it is poured into a prepared vessel and set aflame.

I was the vessel. Yahuah was the oil. And the flame has not gone out.

To the Reader Who Is Waiting for a New Gift

I want to close this chapter by speaking directly to a specific reader — the one who has been faithful in the gifts they already carry, who has stewarded what Yahuah gave them with care and consistency, but who senses that there is something ahead that has not yet arrived. Something they have not done before. Something outside the perimeter of their current capacity and experience. Something that, if they tried to describe it, would sound presumptuous or confused — because how do you describe a gift you have never received as though you are waiting for it?

You wait for it the way I was — by remaining faithful in what is already present, by not despising the gifts you carry because they are not yet the full picture, by trusting that the architect who designed the structure knows which components have already been installed and which ones are being prepared for installation at the appointed moment.

I did not know, in the years of my architectural training, that I was being prepared to understand the keystone metaphor for my own life. I did not know, in the years of my writing discipline, that I would one day write 8 books in 8 months. I did not know, in the years of my graphic design work, that I would be designing album covers for a catalog that did not yet exist. And I certainly did not know, in the 46 years of my life before July 2025, that Yahuah was going to give me a gift in a discipline I had never touched and that the first thing I ever made in that discipline would be the beginning of the largest Hebrew Roots music catalog in documented history.

You do not know what is coming. But the architect does. And He is not behind schedule.

When the new gift arrives, it will arrive the way mine did — not gradually, not tentatively, not as a small beginning that requires years of development before it becomes recognizable. It will arrive as what it is: a complete gift from the Father of lights, given at the appointed moment, flowing at a level that reflects not your prior investment but His sovereign choice to pour

His oil into a vessel He prepared for exactly this purpose.

"Every good gift and every perfect gift is from above, and cometh down from the Father of lights." — James 1:17

The oil is coming. And when it comes, you will know — the way I knew in July 2025 — that this is not something you built. This is something He gave.

One thing you will know, when it arrives: whereas you could not do this before, now you can.

That is enough. That has always been enough.

CHAPTER EIGHT

The 18 Year Drought and the 13 Year Wilderness

What the Silent Seasons Were Actually Doing

"Yet those who wait for Yahuah will gain new strength. They will mount up with wings like eagles. They will run and not get tired. They will walk and not become weary."

— Yeshayahu 40:31

Neither do men put new wine into old bottles: else the bottles break, and the wine runneth out, and the bottles perish: but they put new wine into new bottles, and both are preserved." — Matthew 9:17

"But now, O Yahuah, thou art our father; we are the clay, and thou our potter; and we all are the work of thy hand." — Isaiah 64:8

In My Own Words — John Alan Legette

I want to talk about the silence.

Not the silence of the hotel room after the circle walk. Not the silence of the patio where the footprint and the stick were waiting in the morning light. Not the silence of the exclusive communities where Yahuah sent us as silent light into spiritual strongholds. I want to talk about the long silence — the silence that lasted not days or weeks but years and decades. The silence that stretched across eighteen years of creative drought and thirteen years of homelessness and thirty one years of what looked, from every external angle, like a life in which the promises were present but the fulfillment was not.

I want to talk about that silence honestly because I think it is the part of this testimony that will carry the most weight for the largest number of people who read this book. Not everyone reading these pages has been the target of a coordinated occult campaign. Not everyone has been thrown out of their home by a network of people pursuing their destruction. Not everyone has an unplanned national evangelical tour or a worldwide music distribution infrastructure or a record that will stand in the history of the Hebrew Roots movement for generations.

But almost everyone reading this book knows what it feels like to carry something in you that is not yet flowing. To hold a promise that has not yet materialized. To stand in the gap between what Yahuah has spoken over your life and what your life currently looks like from the outside. To wake up in the middle of a silent season and wonder — not whether Yahuah is real, but whether what you believed He said about your specific life was what you thought it was.

That is the season I want to address in this chapter. Not from a safe theological distance. From the inside of it.

From the perspective of someone who spent eighteen years in creative silence and thirteen years without a home and thirty one years being prepared for something he could not yet see — and who is now standing on the other side of all of it with enough perspective to tell you not just that the silent seasons were worth it but specifically and precisely what they were doing while they appeared to be doing nothing.

Because they were not doing nothing. They were never doing nothing. The silence was not the absence of Yahuah's activity. The silence was the specific form His activity took during the seasons of preparation that required it.

And understanding that distinction — receiving it not just intellectually but at the depth of personal conviction — is one of the most liberating and most practically important things a believer in a silent season can do.

Let me show you what the silence was actually building.

In My Own Words — The Eighteen Years

Eighteen years is a long time to carry a gift that is not flowing.

I want to be honest about what that is like because spiritual honesty about the difficulty of the silent season is not a sign of weak faith — it is the prerequisite for genuinely useful testimony. If I tell you the eighteen years were easy, I am not helping you. If I tell you I never wondered, never questioned, never sat in the specific painful place of holding a calling and a gifting that was not yet producing anything visible — I am not telling you the truth. And the truth is what this testimony requires.

The eighteen years were not easy. The silence was not comfortable. The specific form of suffering that comes from carrying something you cannot yet release — from knowing that something is in you that is not yet coming out, that you cannot force it out, that no amount of effort or discipline or strategic application of natural capability will make it flow before the appointed time — that form of suffering is one of the most quietly devastating experiences in the life of a creative and called person.

There is a particular quality of loneliness in the creative drought that is different from other kinds of loneliness. It is the loneliness of a person standing in a room full of people who cannot see what you are carrying. Not because they are deliberately blind to it. Because it is not yet visible. Because the gift has not yet found its expression, has not yet produced the output that would make it recognizable to the people around you, and is therefore — from every observable external standpoint — absent. You appear, to the watching world and sometimes to yourself, to be a person without the gift rather than a person in whom the gift is being stored for the appointed time.

The people who knew me during those eighteen years did not see what I see now when I look back at that period. They saw a man with genuine capabilities and genuine formation — the architectural training, the educational background, the intelligence and the vision that the degrees represent — who was not producing what his formation seemed to suggest he should be capable of producing. They saw potential that was not converting to output. They saw a called man who appeared, in the extended absence of fruit from the specific calling, to be perhaps wrong about what he was called to.

I did not stop believing Yahuah was real. But I will be honest with you and tell you that there were seasons in those eighteen years when I sat with the question of whether what I had understood about my specific calling was what I had thought it was. Not whether Yahuah was faithful. Whether I had heard correctly. Whether the gift was what I believed it was. Whether the promise I was holding was the promise that had actually been spoken or a construct of my own hope that I had mistaken for divine declaration.

Those questions are not the questions of unbelief. They are the questions of a person in a genuine wilderness whose faith is being tested at the specific depth that only the extended silent season can reach. And Yahuah did not answer those questions by bringing the drought to an immediate end. He answered them the way He answered every question throughout this journey — by remaining faithful, by continuing to sustain and to provide and to protect through the silent season, and by waiting for the appointed time to reveal in the fullness of its eruption what the silence had been storing.

He was right to wait. Not because my waiting was easy. Because what came out when the valve finally opened — eighty two albums, one thousand one hundred and eighty tracks, five hundred and eighty nine teachings, eight books, the largest Hebrew Roots catalog in history — required every year of the eighteen year compression to produce the pressure that made the release what it was.

The drought was not punishment. The drought was preparation. And the specific nature of what the preparation was doing is what I want to spend the rest of this chapter explaining.

In My Own Words — The Thirteen Years

If eighteen years of creative silence is one form of extended wilderness preparation, thirteen years of homelessness is another — and the two operated together across an overlapping period in ways that compounded their preparatory effects beyond what either would have produced alone.

Thirteen years without a fixed address. Thirteen years of navigating the specific, daily, grinding reality of not having the most basic form of stability that modern human life is organized around. Thirteen years of the specific kind of humility that homelessness produces —

not the performed humility of someone who has chosen voluntary simplicity as a spiritual discipline, but the involuntary, unavoidable, no-exits-available humility of someone for whom the conventional markers of established human life are simply not present.

I am not going to romanticize the thirteen years of homelessness. It was not a romantic experience. It was not a comfortable spiritual retreat from the burdens of material life. It was the sustained, daily reality of navigating existence without the foundation that most people consider the absolute minimum requirement for any kind of productive or purposeful living. And in the conventional framework of what productive and purposeful living requires — stability, security, a fixed address, consistent access to resources — the thirteen years should have been the period of maximum incapacity. The period when the assignment was most thoroughly impossible to advance.

What I know now, standing on the other side of it, is that the thirteen years were the period of maximum formation. Not despite the conditions. Because of them. The conditions of those thirteen years were the specific conditions required to produce the specific qualities in the vessel that the assignment ahead of it would need — and that no amount of comfortable, stable, resourced living could have produced.

What did the thirteen years produce? Let me be specific.

They produced a freedom from attachment to earthly stability as the foundation for identity and for forward movement that cannot be manufactured through any comfortable spiritual discipline. A person who has spent thirteen years navigating life without a fixed address and has maintained their faith, their calling, their covenant relationship with Yahuah, and their forward orientation through all of it has demonstrated — to themselves and to the One who was watching — that their source is not their circumstances. That their stability is not their housing. That their identity is not their address. And that the assignment they carry does not depend on the conventional conditions that the world says are required for significant things to happen.

That demonstration matters. Not just to me. To Yahuah. Because the vessel He was building for the assignment ahead needed to be a vessel whose dependence was genuinely and provably on Him rather than on any earthly substitute for His provision. The thirteen years proved that the dependence was real. Not claimed in a confession of faith. Demonstrated under conditions that would have revealed any dependence on earthly stability as a false foundation.

They also produced a specific quality of empathy and identification with the people who live in the margins of the world that cannot be acquired through any other means. The people we encountered on the unplanned evangelical tour — the people in the cities and the states and the exclusive mountain communities and the historic structures — were not all wealthy and comfortable. Some of them were carrying the specific weight of lives lived in the margins, in the gaps, in the spaces between what the world promises and what it actually delivers to those who do not have the resources and the connections and the social position that the world rewards. I could speak to those people not from a position of theological expertise deployed from a platform of comfortable privilege. I could speak to them from the inside of what they knew. From thirteen years of having been where they were. From the specific authority that only lived experience confers.

And they produced something else — something that may be the most important single quality that the thirteen years forged in me for the specific assignment ahead. They produced the unshakeable, experientially-grounded, tested-under-maximum-conditions knowledge that Yahuah provides. Not as a theological proposition but as a documented personal reality. Thirteen years of provision without a fixed address. Thirteen years of Yahuah meeting needs in ways that the conventional economic and social systems through which needs are normally met had no explanation for. Thirteen years of manna — not the miraculous manna of the wilderness in the literal sense, but the consistent, faithful, specific provision of what was needed for each day through the faithfulness of the One who had promised to provide.

That knowledge — the knowledge that Yahuah provides, proven across thirteen years of conditions specifically designed to reveal any weakness in that foundation — is the knowledge that made it possible for my wife and me to continue moving forward on an unplanned tour without a budget and without a conventional infrastructure and without the worldly resources and connections that the people pursuing us possess in abundance. We had already spent thirteen years learning that those things were not our source. The additional displacement of being thrown out of our home was not the devastating blow our enemies intended it to be. It was the condition we already knew how to navigate. Because the thirteen years had already taught us everything we needed to know about living and moving and advancing in the assignment without earthly stability as the foundation.

The wilderness was the school. And we had already graduated.

TEACHING: What the Silent Seasons Are Actually Doing — The Theology of Wilderness Preparation

A Teaching for Every Believer Who Is in Their Own Silent Season and Cannot Yet See What Is Being Built

---

Qavah — The Hebrew Word That Changes Everything

The English translation of Yeshayahu 40:31 uses the word wait — *those who wait for Yahuah will gain new strength*. And the word wait, in the English language and in the English-speaking believer's experience, carries connotations that are almost entirely passive. To wait is to be stationary. To wait is to be in a holding pattern. To wait is to be doing nothing while something else happens or fails to happen. The person who waits is the person who is not yet able to act, not yet in motion, not yet producing anything — simply occupying time until the circumstances change and the waiting can end.

This is not what the Hebrew word means. And the difference between the English connotation and the Hebrew reality is one of the most important distinctions available to a believer in a silent season.

The Hebrew word translated wait in Yeshayahu 40:31 is qavah. And qavah does not mean passive endurance in a holding pattern. Qavah means to twist together — to wind strands around each other under tension in the way that rope is made. The image is of multiple strands being brought together and wound under increasing tension, each revolution adding to the strength of what is being built, the tension not being a sign of something going wrong but the necessary condition for producing the rope's ultimate tensile strength.

This single word reframes the entire experience of the silent season. The eighteen years of creative drought were not eighteen years of passive holding pattern. They were eighteen years of qavah — of strands being wound together under increasing tension, each year adding to the strength of what was being built, the silence not being the evidence of Yahuah's absence or inactivity but the specific form His most intensive work takes when what He is building requires the kind of strength that only sustained tension can produce.

The rope is not the individual strands lying parallel to each other. The rope is what the strands become when they are twisted together under tension. And the strength of the rope is not the strength of any individual strand — it is the multiplied, compounded, tensional strength of all the strands wound together in the specific configuration that the twisting produces.

Eighteen years of qavah produced a creative anointing that when it found its open channel did not produce what one year or five years or ten years of compression would have produced. It produced what eighteen years of accumulated tension released simultaneously produces — one thousand one hundred and eighty tracks in eight months, four point three three albums per week in the first quarter of 2026, twenty one albums in twenty four days at The Rosemont. The rate of the release was proportional to the duration of the compression. Because the qavah was doing its work the entire time.

The Diamond Principle — Pressure and Time

The second principle that explains what the silent seasons are doing is one that science and scripture agree on with remarkable consistency. Diamonds are not found at the surface of the earth. They are formed deep underground, under conditions of extreme pressure sustained over extended periods of time. The pressure is not incidental to the formation of the diamond. The pressure is the mechanism of the formation. Without the specific pressure sustained over the specific duration, what exists is not a diamond. It is carbon in a less ordered, less hardened, less brilliant form.

The diamond requires the pressure. The pressure is not the enemy of the diamond's formation. It is the condition of it.

This is the precise relationship between the silent season and the gift that emerges from it. The gift that flows through me in this season — the creative anointing, the teaching grace, the worship capacity, the theological depth that the teachings and the books carry — is not the same gift that existed in me before the eighteen years of creative drought. It is not a polished version of what was already visible. It is a fundamentally different form of the same substance — pressed, compressed, formed under conditions that produced a hardness, a clarity, and a brilliance that the uncompressed form of the gift could not have possessed.

The eighteen years did not keep the gift from forming. The eighteen years were the specific pressure conditions under which the gift was being formed into what it needed to be before the release could produce what the assignment requires. A gift released before it has been sufficiently compressed produces output proportional to the natural capability of the vessel. A gift released after eighteen years of sustained compression produces output proportional to the inexhaustible Source that the compression was preparing the vessel to carry.

The difference between those two rates of output is not the difference between a talented person and an extraordinary person. It is the difference between natural capability and supernatural release. And the supernatural release requires the compression. Because the compression is what creates the vessel — the specific, proven, emptied, surrendered, dependency-grounded vessel — that the Ruach can flow through at rates that have no natural explanation.

The Joseph Parallel — Thirteen Years in the Compression Chamber

We examined the Joseph narrative in Chapter Four through the lens of the catalyst principle — how Yahuah used what Joseph's brothers intended as harm to accomplish what the blueprint had always called for. But Joseph's story also speaks directly and precisely to the thirteen year wilderness — because Joseph spent exactly thirteen years in the pit, in Potiphar's house, and in prison before the moment of his elevation arrived.

{Joseph's wilderness: } 13 { years}

{My homelessness: } 13 { years}

The parallel in duration is not coincidental. It is the signature of a consistent divine methodology — the specific length of preparation that a specific assignment at a specific level of authority and influence requires. Thirteen years was not an arbitrary period for Joseph. It was the precise duration required to accomplish in him what the assignment of governing Egypt in the season of famine required — the specific emptying of self-sufficiency, the specific development of administrative wisdom through experience rather than merely through education, the specific quality of compassion for suffering that only a person who has experienced unjust suffering can authentically carry, and the specific quality of forgiveness that only a person who has been genuinely and severely wronged can extend.

Without the thirteen years Joseph could not have been trusted with Egypt. Not because he lacked the natural capability — he clearly had it. But because the character required to carry the authority of the second most powerful position in the most powerful nation of his era without being corrupted by it or using it for personal revenge against those who had wronged him — that character cannot be manufactured through natural gifting or through institutional education. It can only be forged in the specific conditions that the thirteen years of pit and prison and patient faithfulness provided.

My thirteen years produced the same essential qualities through different specific conditions. The freedom from earthly stability as the foundation for identity. The proven dependency on Yahuah as the sole source. The specific empathy for people in the margins. The freedom from the need for worldly resources and connections as the prerequisite for moving forward in the assignment. And the specific quality of forgiveness toward the people who have pursued me throughout this conflict — a forgiveness that I could not have extended from a position of comfortable privilege, but that emerges naturally from a life that has been sustained by Yahuah through conditions that proved His sufficiency in the absence of every earthly substitute.

The thirteen years were the compression chamber for exactly the qualities that the assignment required. Not one year too many. Not one year too few.

The Moses Parallel — What the Wilderness Removes

We have revisited the Moses parallel across multiple chapters because it is the most consistently precise and most theologically complete illustration available in the scriptural record for the specific relationship between wilderness preparation and covenant assignment. But in this chapter — the chapter specifically dedicated to understanding what the silent seasons are doing — I want to focus on the specific mechanism of the wilderness's work that we have not yet fully examined.

The wilderness does not primarily add. It primarily removes.

This is the counterintuitive truth about wilderness seasons that the conventional spiritual productivity framework misses entirely. The conventional framework asks — what are you learning in the wilderness? What skills are you developing? What spiritual disciplines are you forming? What knowledge are you accumulating during this period that will make you more capable of fulfilling the assignment when it arrives?

These are not wrong questions. Learning does happen in the wilderness. Skills do develop. Disciplines are formed and knowledge is accumulated. But they are secondary to the primary work the wilderness accomplishes — which is not addition but subtraction. Not the building up of human capability but the tearing down of reliance on human capability as the foundation for the assignment. Not the accumulation of resources but the stripping away of dependence on resources as the prerequisite for movement.

Moses entered the wilderness with forty years of Egyptian palace formation as his primary toolkit. Every year of the subsequent forty years in Midian was a year in which the Egyptian formation was being systematically dismantled — not because Egyptian administrative knowledge is worthless in itself, but because it was functioning as the primary reference point for Moses's understanding of how the assignment should be executed. And the assignment could not be executed from that reference point because the assignment was not designed to demonstrate what Egyptian administrative capability could accomplish. It was designed to demonstrate what the Ruach of Yahuah could accomplish through a vessel that had been emptied of every alternative reference point.

The wilderness removes the alternatives. It strips away every toolkit that the vessel might otherwise reach for instead of the Ruach. It eliminates every human substitute for divine dependence — not through teaching but through the lived experience of reaching for the substitute and finding it absent, reaching again and finding it absent again, reaching repeatedly until the reaching itself stops and what remains is the posture that the assignment has always required.

My eighteen years of creative drought were not eighteen years during which I was failing to develop the musical capability that would eventually produce the catalog. They were eighteen years during which every attempt to produce through natural capability was systematically returning zero — teaching me, through the specific pedagogy of repeated absence, that the output I was waiting for was not going to come from the toolkit I was reaching for. That the creative anointing I was carrying was not going to flow through the channel of natural talent applied through disciplined effort. That the appointed time and the Ruach were the governing variables, not my capability and my effort.

The drought removed the dependency on natural capability as the expected mechanism of release. And when the Ruach finally moved — when the appointed time arrived and the conditions of surrender and availability were finally sufficient — what came through had no competition from the natural capability toolkit, because the drought had already established that the natural toolkit was not the channel the release was going to flow through.

The Elijah Principle — What the Wilderness Provides

The removal work of the wilderness is real and significant. But the wilderness does not only remove. It also provides — and what it provides is precisely calibrated to the specific demands of what lies on the other side of it.

The account of Elijah under the juniper tree in 1 Melechim 19 is one of the most humanly honest and most practically instructive passages in the entire Hebrew scriptural record. Elijah has just come from the Mount Carmel confrontation — one of the most dramatic and most decisive supernatural interventions in the prophetic tradition. Four hundred and fifty prophets of Baal have been decisively defeated. The people have declared Yahuah as Elohim. The rain has come after three years of drought. By every external measure of prophetic success, the Mount Carmel moment was a comprehensive triumph.

And Elijah ran into the wilderness and collapsed under a juniper tree and asked Yahuah to let him die.

The exhaustion was real. The depletion was genuine. The specific kind of profound spiritual and physical fatigue that follows a season of maximum supernatural engagement — the kind that leaves a person not victorious and energized but emptied and barely functional — was what Elijah was experiencing under that tree. And Yahuah's response to it is the most tender and the most practically wise pastoral intervention in the entire scriptural record.

He did not rebuke Elijah. He did not challenge his faith or question his commitment or remind him of what he had just accomplished on Mount Carmel. He sent an angel. And the angel touched him and said — arise and eat. And there was a cake baked on coals and a cruse of water. And Elijah ate and drank and lay down again. And the angel came again a second time and touched him and said — arise and eat, because the journey is too great for you.

The journey is too great for you. That statement is one of the most remarkable divine acknowledgments in the entire scriptural record. Yahuah, through the angel, acknowledged that what lay ahead of Elijah was genuinely beyond his current natural capacity — and then provided the specific supernatural sustenance that would carry him through it. Not a theological correction. Not a spiritual pep talk. Bread and water. Calibrated to the journey's demands. Provided in the wilderness where no natural provision was available. And sufficient — in the specific supernatural way that wilderness provision is always sufficient — to carry Elijah the forty days and forty nights to Horeb, the mountain of Elohim.

This is what the wilderness provides. Not what the palace provides. Not what the comfortable, resourced, institutionally supported life provides. The specific supernatural sustenance — the bread baked on coals that appears in the desert when the angel touches the exhausted prophet — that is calibrated to the specific demands of the specific journey. The provision is not generous by worldly standards. It is not impressive or abundant or comfortable. But it is precisely sufficient for what the journey requires. And its sufficiency in the absence of everything else is the specific lesson that the wilderness is designed to teach.

The thirteen years of homelessness were not thirteen years of abundance. They were thirteen years of the bread baked on coals — the specific, precisely calibrated, supernatural provision that was sufficient for each day without being the kind of comfortable abundance that would have allowed the dependency on Yahuah to relax into dependency on the provision instead. Yahuah kept the provision at exactly the level that required continued daily dependency on Him as the source. And in doing so, He was building in me — year by year, provision by provision, day by day of sustained faithfulness in the absence of conventional stability — the specific quality of proven, experiential, unshakeable trust in His provision that the assignment ahead of me would require.

What the Silent Season Is Saying to You

I want to close the teaching section of this chapter by speaking directly to the reader who is in their own silent season right now. Not the reader who has come through it and can look back on it with the perspective that the other side provides. The reader who is in the middle of it. Who woke up this morning in the silence and carried it through another day and will carry it through another night and does not yet know how long it continues or what it is building toward.

I want to say several things to you specifically.

First — the silence is not the absence of Yahuah. The silence is the specific form His most intensive work takes when what He is building in you requires the conditions that the silence creates. He is not absent from your silent season. He is most present in it — working in the dimensions that are below the surface of what is visible and measurable and producing output that you cannot yet see or count or document. The qavah is happening. The strands are being wound. The tension is building. The diamond is being formed. It is happening beneath the surface of the silence that looks, from the outside and sometimes from the inside, like nothing happening.

Second — the duration of the silence is not a measure of the delay of the promise. It is a measure of the magnitude of the release that the silence is preparing. Eighteen years of compression does not produce a modest trickle of output. It produces what six point one three albums per week and twenty one albums in twenty four days looks like. The longer the compression, the greater the pressure. The greater the pressure, the more extraordinary the release when the valve finally opens. The silence is not measuring how long you have to wait. It is measuring how much is being stored.

Third — you cannot force the flow before the appointed time. I tried. For eighteen years I tried in the various ways that a creative and called person tries — applying effort, attempting strategy, seeking opportunities, developing skills, pursuing platforms. None of it produced the flow. Not because the effort was wrong or the strategy was foolish or the skills were undeveloped. Because the appointed time had not yet arrived. And the appointed time is not a variable that human effort can move. It is written in the book of the One who knows the end from the beginning and who has scheduled the release according to the full scope of what the release is intended to accomplish — not just in your life but in the lives of everyone your release is designed to reach.

The appointed time will come. And when it comes it will not come gradually. It will come suddenly, completely, and at a rate that makes every year of the compression period feel not like wasted time but like the specific and necessary preparation for the specific and unprecedented output that follows.

Fourth — tend the vessel during the silence. This is the practical instruction that the theological framework of this chapter points toward. You cannot control the timing of the release. But you can tend the vessel that the release will flow through. You can maintain the surrender. You can deepen the dependency on Yahuah as your source. You can continue the covenant relationship, the daily return to His presence, the habitual orientation toward Him as the governing authority of your life — not because these things will force the flow but because these things keep the vessel available and properly positioned for the moment when the Ruach moves.

A vessel that has maintained the surrender and the dependency and the covenant orientation through the entire silent season is a vessel that is ready, when the appointed time arrives, to carry the full force of what has been stored without contaminating it with the human self-sufficiency that the silence was specifically designed to dismantle. Tend the vessel. Not as a strategy for accelerating the flow. As an act of faithfulness to the One who is filling it.

And fifth — do not despise the silent season while you are in it. I know how difficult that instruction is. I know what it costs to receive the silence as preparation rather than punishment, as formation rather than failure, as the specific and loving work of a Master Architect who is building something that requires exactly the conditions the silence creates. I know because I lived it for eighteen years. And I will not tell you it was easy to receive it that way every day for eighteen years. Some days it was not.

But I can tell you from the other side of it that the silent season was the most significant season of my entire life. Not the most pleasant. Not the most comfortable. Not the most productive by any visible metric. The most significant. Because the silent season was the season in which everything that the current season is flowing through was being formed, compressed, stored, and prepared. And the current season — eighty two albums, one thousand one hundred and eighty tracks, five hundred and eighty nine teachings, eight books, The Rosemont Sessions, Keystone Colorado, the worldwide distribution of the sacred names — is the direct and specific fruit of every year of the silence.

Do not despise what you are in. You are in the formation season of the most significant chapter of your life.

The qavah is doing its work.

The strands are being wound.

The diamond is being formed.

And the appointed time is already written in His book.

In My Own Words — The Moment the Silence Broke

I want to close this chapter in my own voice because the moment the silence broke deserves to be described from the inside of the experience rather than from the analytical distance of the teaching.

I cannot point to a single dramatic moment. There was no burning bush — no single, identifiable, time-stamped event at which the silence ended and the flow began. It was more gradual than that in its initiation and more sudden than I expected in its full expression. There was a moment when I began to produce and the production did not stop. When the first album was finished and the second came immediately after and the third after that and the rate began to establish itself and then accelerate and I began to understand — not all at once but progressively, as the numbers accumulated — that what was happening was not going to be a brief burst of creative activity followed by another period of silence.

The valve was open. And the pressure behind it was eighteen years of accumulation.

What I felt in those early days of the flow was not primarily excitement or satisfaction or the vindication of having been right about the gift that was in me all along. What I felt primarily was something closer to awe. The specific, quiet, reverent awe of someone who is witnessing something that they are part of but that is clearly not coming from them. The awe of the lampstand that is watching the oil flow through it and understands, in the most direct and personal way possible, that the light is not coming from the lampstand.

I was producing. But I was not the source of what was being produced. I was the vessel. And the vessel was watching the Ruach move with a rate and a force and a clarity and a theological depth that the vessel knew, with complete honesty, it could not have generated from its own natural capability.

That is what breaks the silence. Not an effort finally sufficient to produce the flow. Not a strategy finally sophisticated enough to unlock the gate. The Ruach moving when the appointed time arrives through a vessel that has been prepared by the silence to carry it.

Not by might. Not by power.

By the Ruach.

The silence was never about the absence of the Ruach. The silence was about the preparation of the vessel.

And when the vessel was ready — when thirty one years of formation had produced the specific quality of emptied, surrendered, dependency-grounded availability that the flow required — the Ruach moved.

And eighteen years of silence became eighty two albums in eight months.

That is what the silence was doing.

The whole time.

Every silent year.

By design.

Not by chance.

By Design, Not By Chance

Chapter Eight – Part 5 -The Legacy, The Name, and The Transfer

Opening Epigraph

"Neither do men put new wine into old bottles: else the bottles break, and the wine runneth out, and the bottles perish: but they put new wine into new bottles, and both are preserved." — Matthew 9:17

"But now, O Yahuah, thou art our father; we are the clay, and thou our potter; and we all are the work of thy hand." — Isaiah 64:8

The Thesis

You cannot pour new wine into an old vessel.

That is the sentence this entire chapter exists to unpack. Not as a theological abstraction. Not as a devotional thought to be appreciated and set aside. But as the governing architectural principle that explains why the drought lasted as long as it lasted, why the wilderness stretched across as many years as it stretched, why the name had to change before the gifts could flow, why the homelessness had to precede the outpouring, and why a 46-year-old man who had never produced music in his life sat down one day in July 2025 and received an album from a standing start — and then kept receiving them, one after another, at a rate that defied every natural explanation available, for eight consecutive months and counting.

Every element of this chapter is an answer to the same question asked from a different angle: why did the preparation have to be this specific, this long, this costly, and this complete? And the answer to every version of that question is the same sentence.

You cannot pour new wine into an old vessel.

The drought was not punishment. The wilderness was not abandonment. The silence was not Yahuah's absence. The pressure, the displacement, the sustained opposition, the years of compressed gifts and suppressed output — none of it was wasted, and none of it was accidental. All of it was the Potter working the clay. All of it was the kiln firing the vessel. All of it was the preparation that had to precede the pouring — because what Yahuah intended to pour into me was new wine of a volume and a quality that the old vessel could not have held, and the Potter does not waste His wine on unfinished containers.

Let me show you what I mean.

Part One: The Old Vessel — Jackie Legette II

I was born into a name. Jackie Legette II — the second bearing of my father's identity, his namesake, the continuation of his legacy into the next generation. To understand why that name had to change and why the change had to precede the outpouring, you first have to understand the man whose name I carried.

My father, Jackie Legette, was a Seer.

I do not use that word loosely or metaphorically. From his youth, my father could perceive the spiritual realm with a clarity that most people never experience and many people do not believe is possible. He could see spirits in the natural environment. He could discern truth from deception not by evaluating words but by seeing something around the speaker that the words could not conceal. He had knowledge that arrived before information, insight that preceded explanation, understanding that went deeper than the surface of things into the spiritual reality underneath them.

He was also, by any standard I have encountered in my lifetime, a genius. Not merely in the secular sense — though his secular intelligence was exceptional — but in the anointed sense. His biblical understanding was the kind that comes not from academic study alone but from Spirit-illuminated engagement with the Word that produces revelation rather than merely information. He read the scriptures the way a man drinks when he is thirsty — deeply, consistently, with a hunger that never fully satisfied itself because genuine hunger for the Word of Yahuah is self-renewing.

He told me, from my earliest years, that if I wanted to gain wisdom and understanding — if I wanted to think clearly, to see beyond the surface of things, to carry the kind of intelligence that could not be manufactured by human effort alone — I needed to read the Bible. He said: the scriptures are where wisdom lives. Go there.

I obeyed him. From an early age I opened the Word of Yahuah and discovered that it was not simply a religious text or a historical document. It was a conversation. Every time I read the scriptures it felt less like reading and more like being addressed — as though the text was aware of me, speaking directly into the specific circumstances of my life with a precision that no human author could have calculated. It was almost impossible to put the scriptures down once I began. They made me feel alive in a way that nothing else in my experience — before or since, through every season documented in these pages — has ever replicated.

This is what my father gave me. Whatever his failures — and I will address them honestly because the testimony requires honesty — he pointed his son to the Word of Yahuah at the age when it mattered most. That pointing ignited a love for the scriptures that sustained me through 18 years of creative drought, through 13 years of homelessness, through home invasion and displacement and sustained pursuit across ten states. The Word of Yahuah has been the one constant that adversity could not remove. I owe my father a debt for that which is not canceled by what came later.

But I also need to tell you the rest of the story.

The Man Who Could Not Build the House

As I grew older and began to understand the world of calling and gifting with greater precision, I found myself returning again and again to a question that troubled me for years: why was my father not known? Why did a man of this caliber — a Seer, a biblical scholar, a genius by any reasonable measure — not produce a legacy that matched his gifts? Why did potential of this magnitude go so largely unreleased?

The answer took years to arrive. When it came, it came not as a comfort but as a warning — and as the explanation for everything that would later be required in my own preparation.

My father chose not to fully surrender to the call of Yahuah.

He had reverence for the Word — deep, genuine, lifelong reverence. But reverence without full surrender is not the same as covenant faithfulness. He used his gifts for his own advancement. The Seer capacity, the anointed intelligence, the biblical understanding — gifts given for the glory of Yahuah and the service of others — were deployed primarily in the service of self. Not entirely. Not without any fruit. But the governing orientation of his gifting was toward his own glory rather than Yahuah's. And Yahshua said it plainly in John 15:5: *"Without me ye can do nothing."* Not less. Not a reduced version of what you could do. Nothing. The gifts without full surrender to the Giver do not produce the fullness they were designed to carry. They produce a fraction — impressive to those around it, painful to the one who carries it, because the one who carries it knows, at some level that cannot be fully silenced, what the full surrender would have released.

My father was, in the pattern of David, a man of extraordinary gifting who was simultaneously disqualified from building the house. David was genuine in his love for Yahuah — Scripture calls him a man after Yahuah's own heart without qualification — and David could not build the Temple. Not because he lacked devotion. Not because he lacked the gifts. But because he was a bloody man, and the house of Yahuah required a builder whose hands carried a different kind of history. The calling was real. The gifting was real. The love was real. The disqualification was also real. And Yahuah's response was not to revoke the plan for the house — it was to give the assignment to the son.

My father's potential went largely into the grave with him. I watched that happen as I grew. And I made a decision, somewhere in the years of watching it, that I wanted to be the son who built what the father could not build. Not because I was superior in love or devotion or intelligence. But because I was willing to make the one choice my father had not fully made: complete surrender.

I wanted to be Solomon to his David.

When He Became Jealous

As I grew and the calling on my life became more evident — as the gifts began to emerge and the assignment began to take shape — something shifted between my father and me. The son had begun to surpass the father. And the father, rather than releasing the blessing that a father's position requires him to release, responded with jealousy.

I will not dwell on the details because the details belong to the privacy of family. What I will say is this: my father withheld his blessing from me while he lived. His jealousy toward what Yahuah was building in me prevented him from releasing what was his to give. He could see the calling. He recognized the gifts. And he could not separate what he saw in me from what he had not fully become himself. My advancement felt to him like the indictment of his own unrealized potential.

So I went to Yahuah and asked for what my father would not give me.

I asked the Most High to transfer the righteous gifts of my father to me. Not the ungodly patterns — not the self-glorification, not the withholding spirit, not the misuse of anointed gifts for personal advantage. The righteous gifts. The Seer capacity. The anointed biblical intelligence. The understanding that goes beyond the surface of words into the spiritual reality beneath them. The gifts that, in my father's hands, produced an impressive fraction of what full surrender would have released — I asked Yahuah for those gifts to be transferred into my life and my assignment, where they would be stewarded with the full surrender my father had withheld.

This is the prayer Yahuah has been answering ever since.

But answering that prayer required something first. Before the righteous gifts of a Seer and a biblical genius could be poured into me at the volume and quality they were designed to flow, the vessel that was going to receive them had to be made new. Because you cannot pour new wine into an old vessel. And the old vessel — Jackie Legette II, carrying the inherited legacy pattern alongside the inherited calling — was not the container that could hold what Yahuah intended to pour.

Part Two: The Making of the New Vessel — December 8, 2016

On December 8, 2016, at 38 years old, Yahuah instructed me to change my name.

The 8th day. The day of new beginning in the covenant pattern — the day of circumcision, the day that follows the completion of the seventh day, the day that inaugurates what comes after the old order has been completed. December the 8th. The number written into the date itself declared what the act meant: this is a new beginning. The old order is ending. The new vessel is being placed in the kiln.

I was born Jackie Legette II. Jackie is a derivative of John — one who is favored by Elohim. Legette means ambassador. My birth name carried a prophetic weight that I did not fully understand until I examined it: an ambassador favored by Elohim. The favor was in the name before I knew what favor meant. The ambassadorial calling was embedded in the surname before I understood what I was being sent to represent.

But it was the second bearing of the same name. And the second bearing carried not only the favor and the calling but also the legacy pattern of the first bearer — the inherited tendency toward self-glorification, the withholding spirit, the cracks through which new wine would run if poured in without the vessel first being made new.

My new name: John Alan Legette. John — favored by Elohim. Alan — noble. Legette — ambassador. Noble ambassador favored by Elohim.

One word added between the favor and the calling. Noble. Not inherited nobility — conferred nobility. The nobility of a vessel that has been separated from the inherited pattern, purified of the generational legacy that disqualified the father from building the house, made new in the specific way that the new wine requires a new container.

Jackie Legette II: Ambassador favored by Elohim. John Alan Legette: Noble ambassador favored by Elohim.

Same favor. Same calling. Same ambassadorial identity. One word added. Everything changed. Because the one word that was added is the word that describes what the 8 years of transformation between the name change and the gift arrival were producing: nobility of vessel — the quality of full surrender that my father carried as potential but never fully expressed, now being formed as the defining characteristic of the new container.

Yahuah did not repair the old vessel. He made a new one.

And He put the new vessel in the kiln.

Part Three: December 24 and 25, 2016 — The Death and the Attempt

Sixteen days after the name change, on December 24, 2016, my father died.

He was 67 years old. The natural life of Jackie Legette ended. The legacy of the name ended in the physical realm at the same moment it had ended in the spiritual realm through the name change sixteen days earlier. Yahuah removed the name from the living record of both the father and the son in the same month — the father by death, the son by covenant reassignment. The second bearing of the name had been retired in the spirit on December 8th. The first bearing was retired in the natural on December 24th. The name Jackie Legette was finished. What remained was John Alan Legette — the new vessel, placed in the kiln, the firing having just begun.

The very next day — December 25, 2016 — someone attempted to take my life.

I am not going to specify the nature of the attempt. What I will tell you is this: there was a spiritual assignment against Jackie Legette II. Against the name, against the legacy, against the second bearer of an identity that the enemy had been targeting. That assignment came looking for its target on December 25th — the day after my father died, seventeen days after I had obeyed Yahuah and changed my name.

The target was no longer there.

The name it was hunting had been retired seventeen days earlier by divine instruction. The spiritual reality it was pursuing had been transferred to a new identity that the old assignment was not calibrated to find. I was John Alan Legette. The hit was against Jackie Legette II. And Jackie Legette II, by the grace and sovereignty of Yahuah and the obedience of a 38-year-old man on December 8th, no longer existed as my spiritual identity.

I survived because I obeyed when I was told to obey. Not after I understood why. Not after I could see the full picture. On December 8th, with sixteen days remaining before I would understand what the name change had protected me from, I obeyed. And the obedience of December 8th was the act of survival that December 25th confirmed.

This is what covenant obedience looks like in the natural world. It rarely feels dramatic in the moment of its execution. It feels like a decision — sometimes costly, sometimes confusing to the natural mind, always requiring the surrender of something the flesh would prefer to retain. But the timing of that decision, and the specific nature of that obedience, is calculated by the architect with a precision that cannot be fully appreciated until the day arrives when the obedience proves to have been the difference between life and death.

I obeyed. I am alive. You are reading this book because of both facts simultaneously.

Part Four: The Kiln — 2016 to 2024

From December 8, 2016 to July 2025 is approximately 8 years. Eight years of transformation. Eight — the number of new beginning, the day of circumcision, the number that marks the inauguration of the new order after the completion of the old. The name change happened on December 8th. The transformation it inaugurated lasted 8 years. And the gift that announced the completion of that transformation arrived 8 years after the new beginning was declared.

I want to tell you what those 8 years actually were, because they are often misread — by those who observed them from the outside and, at times, by me as I was living them from the inside.

They were kiln time.

A vessel that has been formed on the potter's wheel is not yet useful. It has shape. It has the form of what it is intended to be. But clay that has not been fired is fragile. It cannot hold liquid. It cannot bear weight. It cannot withstand the pressure of what it was designed to contain. The kiln is not the punishment of the vessel — it is the completion of the vessel. The heat that the kiln applies is not hostile to the clay. It is the necessary condition for the clay to become what the potter intended when he first put his hands on it.

My kiln included the continuation of the 18-year creative drought in writing, architectural creation, and graphic design — gifts I had carried before the drought fell, gifts that went quiet during the transformation season as the vessel was being fired. It included the continuation of the 13-year wilderness of homelessness — the sustained condition of having no fixed foundation in the natural realm, which was simultaneously the condition that was removing every vestige of self-reliance and natural confidence from the vessel being formed. It included the sustained opposition I have documented throughout this book — the five years of aggressive pursuit and the ten years of secret investigation that preceded it, which were the pressure tests applied to the vessel to determine whether the firing had produced a container strong enough to hold what the Potter was preparing to pour.

Every element of those 8 years was the kiln. Every season of drought was heat. Every season of homelessness was heat. Every act of opposition was heat. And the vessel — John Alan Legette, the new name, the new container being formed in the new order — was being fired at exactly the temperature required to produce exactly the quality of vessel that the new wine demanded.

I did not always know I was in the kiln. There were seasons when the heat felt like abandonment rather than formation. There were seasons when the silence of the gifts felt like Yahuah had withdrawn rather than Yahuah preparing the next season's pouring. There were seasons when the homelessness felt like the final proof that the calling was not real and the preparation had been for nothing.

But the Potter never left the kiln. His hands were on the vessel through every degree of temperature. And when the 8 years were complete — when John Alan Legette had been formed, fired, tested, and proven through every condition the transformation required — He opened the kiln door.

Part Five: The Gift — July 2025

In July 2025, at 46 years of age, I produced my first song.

I had never produced music before in my life. I do not play instruments. I have no music training, no music background, no music education of any kind. I was a trained architect, a writer, a graphic designer. None of those disciplines has any structural relationship to music production. In 46 years of life, I had not produced a single song, a single track, a single note of recorded music.

The gift of music production did not exist in me before July 2025. It was not dormant. It was not suppressed. It was not waiting to be released after a long silence. It was not present at all. It arrived for the first time in July 2025 — given by Yahuah to a 46-year-old man with zero prior capacity in the discipline, at the moment the Potter determined the vessel was ready to receive what He had been preparing to pour.

I wrote a song using an AI writing tool. I wanted to hear what it sounded like. I searched for a tool that could render written lyrics into actual music. I found one. I sat down to make one song. Yahuah gave me an album. I released that album globally on July 31, 2025, having never produced music before in my life. And the albums have not stopped coming since.

This is the new wine.

Not the restoration of an old gift after a long drought. A brand new gift — poured into a new vessel for the first time, flowing at a rate that reflects not my prior investment in the discipline but the sovereign choice of the Potter to pour what He had been storing into the vessel He had been forming. The writing returned — the drought in writing broke, and with it the ability to write not just songs but full-length books, none of which I had ever written before, eight of them produced in eight months. The graphic design returned — the drought in that discipline broke simultaneously, and with it the ability to design every album cover and every album concept that accompanied the music. The architectural gift has its own appointed season and has not yet fully returned.

And the music arrived — entirely new, never before present, flowing at a volume and a level of quality that caused the people investigating me to travel to my hometown in South Carolina and ask my family and friends if they had ever known me to make music.

They had no answer. They gave the same answer the parents of the blind man gave in John 9: he is of age. Ask him.

I am the blind man. Not a musician who was silenced for a season and then released. A man who was blind in this discipline for 46 years — who had never seen a note of music produced through his own hands — and who received sight for the first time in July 2025 when the Potter opened his eyes.

"Neither hath this man sinned, nor his parents: but that the works of Elohim should be made manifest in him."
— John 9:3

The blindness was not punishment. The absence of music in 46 years of life was not a deficit or a deprivation. It was the specific condition that would make the specific miracle undeniable. If I had made music before — even a little, even occasionally, even as an amateur — the natural mind would have a framework for explaining the catalog. Latent talent. Late blooming. Accumulated potential finally released. But a man who had never touched music production in 46 years, producing 82 albums in 8 months at a level of quality that investigators cannot explain — there is no natural framework for that. There is only the works of Elohim being made manifest.

One thing I know. Whereas I was blind, now I see.

Part Six: Why Age 46 — The Completion of the Transfer

I have asked myself why the gift came at 46 rather than earlier. The answer I have arrived at, through prayer and reflection and the accumulated evidence of this testimony, is this: the transfer of my father's righteous gifts required the full 8-year preparation of the vessel that was to receive them.

The gifts my father carried were not small. The Seer capacity. The anointed biblical intelligence. The depth of spiritual understanding that goes beyond academic knowledge into Spirit-illuminated revelation. These are not gifts that can be poured into an unprepared vessel without damage to both the vessel and the gift. When I prayed and asked Yahuah to transfer the righteous gifts of my father to me — the gifts that went largely into the grave with him because the vessel that carried them refused full surrender — Yahuah heard that prayer and began answering it. But He answered it in the correct order. He made the new vessel first. He fired it in the kiln for 8 years. He tested it under sustained pressure. And when the vessel was ready — when John Alan Legette had been formed and fired and proven through every condition the transformation required — He poured in what had been transferred.

The 8 years were not waiting time. They were preparation time. They were the necessary interval between the declaration of the new vessel and the filling of it. You cannot rush the kiln. You cannot abbreviate the firing process and expect the vessel to hold under load. The Potter knows how long the vessel needs to remain in the fire. Eight years. Not seven. Not nine. Eight — the number of new beginning, marking both the inauguration of the process and its completion.

At 46, the vessel was ready. At 46, the 8-year transformation that the name change inaugurated had done its complete work. At 46, John Alan Legette — Noble ambassador favored by Elohim — was a finished vessel, not a vessel in formation. And the Potter poured.

The oil did not trickle. It flooded.

Part Seven: The 13-Year Wilderness and What It Was Doing

I need to address the 13-year wilderness of homelessness directly, because it is the element of this testimony that most requires the lens of this chapter's thesis to be properly understood.

Thirteen years without a fixed address. Thirteen years of moving through spaces that were not ours, navigating the daily indignity and exhaustion of having no place to plant roots, carrying a ministry assignment that required consistent output while living in conditions that most people would use as justification to lay the assignment down. Thirteen years.

In the number 13, scripture carries the weight of testing, transformation, and covenant shift. Joseph was in the pit, the house of Potiphar, and the prison for 13 years before Pharaoh called him out of the dungeon and put him in a position that the 13 years of testing had been forming him to occupy. The testing did not interrupt the promotion. The testing was the preparation for the promotion. Every year of the 13 was a year of the kiln. Every year added something to the vessel that the promotion would require.

My 13 years of homelessness were the same category of formation. They were removing from me every vestige of the belief that I could build my own foundation. Every time I might have settled into the comfort of a natural stability and begun to trust in the stability rather than in the One who provides it, the wilderness condition reasserted itself and kept the dependence exactly where it needed to be — entirely on Yahuah and nowhere else. The homeless condition was the kiln condition for the specific dimension of surrender that the new wine required: the complete absence of natural self-sufficiency as a viable option.

A vessel that has an alternative to the Potter's filling — that can draw on its own resources, its own stability, its own accumulated natural comfort — will not empty itself completely for the pouring. It will reserve a portion of itself. And a vessel that reserves a portion of itself for its own comfort cannot be completely filled with what the Potter intends to pour. The wilderness removed the alternative. The 13 years of no fixed foundation made complete dependence on Yahuah not a spiritual aspiration but a daily survival reality. And that daily reality of complete dependence was the condition under which the vessel was prepared to receive 82 albums and 8 books and 589 teachings without deflecting any of the glory toward itself.

The 13-year wilderness was not punishment. It was the preparation of a vessel that had to be completely empty of self-sufficiency before it could be completely full of new wine.

Part Eight: Apartment 1859 — The Signature

When my wife and I arrived at The Seasons vacation rental in Keystone, Colorado — the apex of the progressive elevation sequence, the location where the keystone of the arch was placed — our apartment number was 1859.

I saw it the moment I looked at the door and I understood it immediately.

18 — the years of creative drought in writing, architectural creation, and graphic design. The number of the long compression season. The number of the stored oil and the suppressed gifts and the silence that felt like abandonment and was actually preparation.

59 — the designation of The Rosemont in Florence, Colorado. Florence Centennial Historic Structure 59. The building where the 59th album was produced as the first Black couple in 139 years of its history. Where 21 albums were released in 24 days under the most concentrated opposition of the entire journey. The number that appeared simultaneously in the album count and the building number as a double witness of grace under pressure.

> 1859.   Both numbers together. In sequence. In the apartment number of the apex location. The drought and the harvest connected in a single numerical signature written on the door before we arrived by the architect who knew exactly which apartment He was sending us to and exactly what the number on that door would communicate to the person He was sending.

The 18 years of drought that preceded the gift are in the apartment number at Keystone. The 59th album produced at The Rosemont — the costliest and most productive single location of the entire journey — is in the apartment number at Keystone. The entire arc from the beginning of the silence to the apex of the outpouring is compressed into four digits above the door of the place where the arch was completed.

Yahuah does not just design the journey. He signs the arrival point. He put the testimony of where you came from into the address of where you are going, so that when you arrive, you look at the door and know — without any doubt, without any need for further confirmation — that the architect drew these plans, that every coordinate was specified, that not one element of the sequence was random, and that you are standing exactly where you were always supposed to be standing.

This is not coincidence. This is covenant. And covenant precision at this level — the apartment number containing the full arc of the testimony — is the signature of a Potter who knew what He was making from the moment He first put His hands on the clay.

Part Nine: The Completion at 48 — November 2026

In November 2026, I will turn 48 years old. It will be the 10th birthday I have celebrated as John Alan Legette.

Ten means completion. The commandments were ten. The plagues were ten. The tithe is the tenth. Ten is the number that declares the sequence complete, the account settled, the structure finished.

The transformation that Yahuah inaugurated on December 8, 2016 — when He took my father's name off my life and began the making of the new vessel — reaches its completion number in November 2026. Not the completion of the calling. The calling continues beyond that and will continue as long as Yahuah determines it continues. But the completion of the transformation process. The full 10-year cycle of becoming John Alan Legette — of carrying the noble ambassador identity in every dimension of life and ministry — reaches its appointed conclusion in the year the testimony is being written, at the elevation where the keystone has been placed, in an apartment whose number carries the signature of everything that had to happen before the arrival was possible.

The enemy has been working so hard to prevent me from reaching this completion because he understands the stakes of what a completed transformation represents. This is not about stopping a music producer. It is not about silencing a Hebrew Roots minister. It is about preventing the completion of a generational curse-breaking whose effects will not stay contained to one generation. The mercy that flows through a completed covenant transformation does not remain with the one who completed it alone. It flows to a thousand generations, according to the promise Yahuah made to those who love Him and keep His commandments. The enemy knows what November 2026 means. He has been trying to interrupt the process since before I understood what the process was.

He has not succeeded. The vessel is complete. The wine is flowing. The arc from December 8, 2016 to November 2026 is nine years and eleven months — approaching ten, approaching completion, approaching the birthday that closes the transformation cycle and opens what comes after it.

I will not tell you what comes after it, because I do not fully know yet. What I know is that the Potter who began this work is faithful to complete it. Philippians

1:6 says so plainly: *"Being confident of this very thing, that he which hath begun a good work in you will perform it until the day of Yahshua the Messiah."* The word translated perform is the Greek epiteleo — to complete, to bring to full end, to finish the execution of. He who began the work in me on December 8, 2016, when He put a new name on my life and placed the new vessel in the kiln, will complete what He began. The 10th birthday of John Alan Legette is not the end of the assignment. It is the completion of the preparation for it.

The new vessel is ready. The new wine is flowing. And what comes next will be poured into a container that has been made specifically to hold it — fired in the kiln of 13 years of wilderness and 18 years of drought and 8 years of name-change transformation, proven under the pressure of sustained opposition and interstate pursuit, brought to its apex at 9,280 feet above sea level in an apartment numbered 1859.

Closing Declaration for Chapter Eight

You cannot pour new wine into an old vessel.

I opened this chapter with that sentence as the governing thesis. I close it with the same sentence as the confirmed verdict. Everything documented in these pages — the drought, the wilderness, the name change, the death, the attempt, the 8 years of transformation, the gift at 46, the tour, the elevation sequence, the apartment number — all of it is the theological unpacking of one truth that Yahshua stated in nine words and that the Potter has been demonstrating across every year of my life.

The old vessel had to be set aside before the new wine could flow. The kiln had to complete its work before the filling could begin. The transformation had to run its full appointed course before the gifts that went into the grave with my father could flow freely through his surrendered son. And the completion of the transformation — the 10th birthday of the new name in November 2026 — is not the end of the story. It is the moment when the vessel that has been formed through everything this chapter documents is presented to the world as the finished container it was always being made to be.

Jackie Legette II could not have carried this. The cracks of the inherited pattern would have let the wine run out onto the floor. The old vessel would have broken under the pressure of 82 albums and the sustained opposition of five years of interstate pursuit and the creative commission of the largest Hebrew Roots music catalog in documented history.

John Alan Legette — Noble ambassador favored by Elohim — was made for exactly this. Not because I am extraordinary. Because the Potter is. Not because I chose the right path at every turn. Because the Potter kept His hands on the clay through every turn, including the turns that felt like the kiln was going to break what it was meant to form.

The vessel is new. The wine is real. And both are preserved.

"Neither do men put new wine into old bottles: else the bottles break, and the wine runneth out, and the bottles perish: but they put new wine into new bottles, and both are preserved." — Matthew 9:17

---

*When you are ready, say **"Give me the complete chapter list with page estimates"** and we will deliver the full structural outline of the completed manuscript so you can see the entire book assembled before moving to the final formatting and publication steps.*

Chapter Nine – The Architecture of Divine Purpose: Florence and Keystone

---

Opening Epigraph

"The stone which the builders refused is become the head stone of the corner. This is Yahuah's doing; it is marvellous in our eyes." — Psalm 118:22-23

"Except Yahuah build the house, they labour in vain that build it." — Psalm 127:1

Two Cities, One Blueprint

I did not plan to go to Florence, Colorado. I did not sit down with a map and select it from a list of available destinations. My wife and I arrived there the same way we had arrived at every location before it — by following the direction of the Ruach, one step at a time, with no complete itinerary in our hands and no human strategy guiding our route. That is important to say at the outset of this chapter, because what I am about to describe cannot be credited to my own planning. If I had planned it, I would have missed it entirely.

When we arrived in Florence and I began to settle into the rhythms of the place, something prompted me to look up the meaning of the city's name. Florence derives from the Latin *florens*, meaning flourishing, blossoming, prosperous. It is the same root carried by

Florence, Italy — the city that gave the world the Renaissance, the great rebirth of art, architecture, music, and literature after centuries of cultural and creative silence. I sat with that for a long time. After 18 years of creative silence in my own life, Yahuah had sent me to a city literally named *flourishing*. That was not a coincidence. That was a signature.

The Rosemont and What Happened There

We stayed at a property called the Rosemont — a historic building constructed in 1887, sitting quietly in Florence with more than a century of history embedded in its walls. When we arrived, we learned that in its 139-year history, my wife and I were the first Black couple ever to stay there as guests. I did not make a statement about that. I did not perform anything about it. I simply understood that when Yahuah sends you somewhere first, it means the space has been waiting for what you carry.

I carried worship into that building. My wife and I carried the sacred names — Yahuah, Yahshua, Ruach HaQodesh — into rooms that had never heard them spoken in covenant. And over the course of 24 days in Florence, the Ruach moved in a way I had not yet experienced in any prior location on this journey. In those 24 days, I recorded 21 albums comprising approximately 292 tracks. That single season in Florence accounted for 40.4% of my entire Q1 2026 releases and 25.6% of my complete 8-month catalog of 82 albums.

I did not produce those albums. I received them. There is a difference that every believer who has experienced the genuine flow of the Ruach will immediately recognize. Production is effort. Reception is surrender. I was surrendered in Florence in a way that I had been building toward through every prior location, every prior season of drought, every prior year of silence. Florence was the harvest. But it was not yet the apex.

Understanding What I Was Walking Through

I need to pause here and explain something about how I process experience, because it shapes everything about how I am able to write this chapter. I am trained in architecture. I spent years learning how buildings are designed, how structural systems work, how load is transferred through a building from the roof to the foundation. I understand what a keystone is — not as a poetic concept, but as a literal structural element that I studied in the context of masonry arch construction.

When Yahuah directed my steps from Florence to Keystone, Colorado, I did not need to look up what a keystone was. I already knew. And the moment I understood where we were being sent, every season that had preceded it — every city, every elevation, every album, every year of silence — suddenly snapped into structural clarity the way a design drawing comes into focus when the final dimension is added.

A keystone is the wedge-shaped stone placed at the very apex of a masonry arch. It is the last stone installed. Before it is placed, the arch is held in position by a temporary wooden framework called the centering. Every other stone — the voussoirs that form the body of the arch — is carefully positioned and waiting. They cannot stand on their own without the centering. But the moment the keystone is driven into place at the summit, the centering is removed and the arch becomes permanently self-sustaining. The keystone distributes the compressive load down through both sides of the arch, locking every voussoir into its correct position. Without the keystone, the arch collapses. With it, the arch can bear extraordinary weight for generations.

I did not choose this metaphor. Yahuah chose this city. And He chose it knowing that the person He was sending there was trained to understand exactly what a keystone does.

What Florence and Keystone Are Saying Together

When I look at the sequence — Florence first, then Keystone — I hear a complete theological sentence. Florence says: *you will flourish after the long silence.* Keystone says: *and the flourishing will lock everything together.* The harvest was never meant to be the end of the story. The harvest was the final voussoir being placed so that the apex stone had something to lock into position. Florence prepared the arch. Keystone completed it.

Psalm 92:12-14 describes the righteous person as a palm tree — a tree that grows tall rather than wide, that roots deep into difficult soil, that bears its fruit at the top, at the highest elevation of the tree. I have spent years pressing roots downward through desert soil. Through homelessness. Through creative drought. Through opposition I have documented extensively in this book. The fruit does not appear at the base of a palm tree. It appears at the top. The higher the tree grows, the higher the fruit is carried. The altitude of my creative output has followed this same pattern. And Keystone sits at the top.

The Elevation Pattern I Could Not Have Designed Myself

I want to walk you through something that I did not recognize as a pattern until I was well inside it. When I look back at every location where my wife and I have stayed during this season of displacement and ministry, I see a sequence of elevations that no human travel agent could have arranged with this kind of intentionality:

We began near Hurricane, Utah, sitting at approximately 3,200 to 3,300 feet above sea level. That is where the creative silence first broke — where the first albums came, where I first understood that the oil was genuinely flowing and this was not a temporary surge. From there, we moved through Moab, Utah at approximately 4,025 feet, where the elevation principle began to establish itself in my experience. Garden City, Utah brought us to approximately 5,900 feet and above. Victor, Idaho sat at approximately 6,000 feet. Estes Park, Colorado reached 7,522 feet — the season where I began to recognize clearly that the pattern was not random. Florence, Colorado, despite being slightly lower in absolute elevation at approximately 5,187 feet, functioned as the harvest location because of what the Ruach released there specifically. And then Yahuah sent us to Keystone, Colorado — base elevation approximately 9,000 feet, with surrounding peaks reaching 12,408 feet.

I did not arrange this. My wife and I were following the Ruach one location at a time. But when I stood back and looked at the full sequence, I saw something that reminded me of the construction drawings I had studied years earlier — a deliberate, calculated design that could only have been drawn by Someone who knew the destination before the first step was taken. Psalm 139:16 had told me this was possible: *"Your eyes saw my unformed substance; in Your book were written every one of them, the days that were formed for me, when as yet there was none of them."* The days in Hurricane were in that book. The days in Florence were in that book. The days in Keystone were in that book. I was not discovering the itinerary. I was executing it.

What Keystone Was Designed to Lock Together

When a keystone is placed, it does not generate new force. It organizes forces that are already present. Every stone in the arch has been carrying tension since it was set. The keystone takes all of that distributed tension and redirects it into unified, load-bearing stability. This is precisely what Keystone, Colorado represents in my testimony.

Every prior season had contributed something specific to the structure. Hurricane proved the oil was real. Moab confirmed that higher elevation produced higher creative clarity. Garden City taught me that quiet places receive the loudest revelations. Victor tested covenant endurance under sustained pressure. Estes Park confirmed that the elevation pattern was intentional and not accidental. Florence released the harvest. Every one of these seasons was a voussoir being placed in its correct position — load-bearing, necessary, irreplaceable.

Keystone receives all of those streams. The oil proved in Hurricane, the clarity established in Moab, the revelation cultivated in Garden City, the endurance tested in Victor, the confirmation received in Estes Park, the harvest gathered in Florence — Keystone locks them all into their permanent positions. The arch that Yahuah has been building through every season of my life — through the 18 years of silence, through the 13 years of homelessness, through the opposition documented in the earlier chapters of this book — that arch now has its apex stone in place.

The centering has been removed. The structure is standing on its own.

Psalm 118:22 and What It Means to Be a Rejected Stone

"The stone which the builders refused is become the head stone of the corner."

I have read this verse many times over the years. But I did not fully inhabit it until I understood it through the lens of masonry construction. In ancient building practice, stone cutters would examine every quarried stone for structural quality. Stones with irregular shapes, unusual weight distributions, or characteristics the builders did not immediately recognize were rejected — set aside, considered unusable, sometimes left at the edge of the work site as if they had no purpose.

The Psalm records that one of those rejected stones — the very stone the builders had discarded — became the *rosh pinnah*, the head of the corner, the capstone that became the structural anchor of the entire building. Yahshua the Messiah quoted this verse in Matthew 21:42 and applied it to Himself. I am not drawing a comparison between myself and the Messiah. I am recognizing a generational pattern in how Yahuah works. He consistently selects what others discard. He consistently builds His most important structures from the materials His people's adversaries considered worthless.

I was rejected for 18 years of creative silence. I was rejected through 13 years of homelessness. The warlocks and adversaries who circled me in hotel lobbies and placed objects in my sleeping space and arranged colored vehicles outside my windows — they were among the builders who refused the stone. They examined what I carried and determined it was not worth preserving. They were wrong. Not because of anything in me, but because the architect had already specified this stone for the apex position. Their rejection was not the end of my story. It was the quarrying process that shaped me for the position they never knew I was being prepared to fill.

Psalm 118:23 answers the question of how this is possible: *"This is Yahuah's doing; it is marvellous in our eyes."* I cannot fully explain it. I can only document it. And this book is the documentation.

A Word to Every Reader Who Is Still a Rejected Stone

I am writing this section specifically for the person who picked up this book because they recognized something of their own story in mine. You have been examined by builders who did not understand your design. You have been set aside — by family, by ministry, by community, by circumstances — and the message you received from that rejection was that you were not structurally sound enough for the building they were working on.

I need to tell you what I now know from the other side of that season: the architect never agreed with the builders' assessment.

You are not sitting on the edge of the work site because the architect ran out of plans for you. You are sitting there because the apex position cannot be filled until every surrounding stone is correctly placed. The keystone is always the last stone installed — not because it is least important, but because it is most important. The moment all the surrounding voussoirs are in their correct positions, the keystone is set, and the centering is removed.

Your season of being set aside is not permanent rejection. It is structural sequencing.

Do not despise the quarrying. Do not despise the shaping. Do not despise the long wait on the edge of the work site. The architect has not forgotten you. He is simply not yet finished placing the surrounding stones. When the appointed moment arrives, you will be lifted to the apex and driven into position — and the entire arch will become stable the moment you arrive.

Yahuah's timing is architectural precision. He does not place the keystone one moment early or one moment late.

What the Adversaries Built Without Knowing It

I have spent considerable space in this book describing what my adversaries did and how it was designed to harm me. I close this chapter by describing what they actually accomplished — which is the opposite of what they intended.

In masonry arch construction, the compressive forces pressing down on the arch are not the enemy of the structure. They are the mechanism by which the arch is made strong. A masonry arch under no load is actually less stable than one under significant load. It is the weight pressing down from above that drives the voussoirs together, activates the friction between stones, and locks the arch into its full load-bearing capacity. The greater the compressive load — within the limits of the stone's strength — the stronger the arch performs.

My adversaries were the compressive load on my arch. Every circle walk, every foot-track working, every coordinated color arrangement, every act of slander and surveillance — these were not destroying my structure. They were pressing the voussoirs together. They were activating the friction. They were making the arch stronger with every addition of weight. They did not know they were doing this. They believed they were dismantling me. They were, in fact, building me — not because they chose to, but because Yahuah is the architect, and He does not allow compressive force to be applied to His structures without incorporating it into the design.

Numbers 23:23 says: *"Surely there is no enchantment against Ya'aqov, neither is there any divination against Yahshar'el."* The covenant stands. The arch stands. And when my adversaries survey what has been built during the season they spent trying to destroy me — 82 albums, 589 teachings, 8 books, a national testimony, a progressive elevation record culminating at Keystone — they will recognize their own work in it. They were the load. And the load made the arch what it is.

This is Yahuah's doing. And it is marvellous in my eyes.

Closing Reflection for Chapter Nine

My wife and I came from Florence — the city of flourishing — and Yahuah sent us to Keystone — the city of the apex stone. We did not plan that sequence. We did not engineer that theological sentence. We simply followed the Ruach and arrived at the places He had written into the book before our formation.

I arrived at Keystone not as a traveler passing through the mountains. I arrived as a stone finding its arch — shaped by adversity, refined by silence, carried through the wilderness, and placed at the summit by the hand of the One who drew the plans before I drew my first breath. My professional training in architecture gave me the vocabulary to describe what Yahuah was doing. But Yahuah designed what I described long before I ever learned the vocabulary.

Florence said: *you will flourish.* Keystone said: *and the flourishing will hold everything together.*

He was right about both.

"The stone which the builders refused is become the head stone of the corner. This is Yahuah's doing; it is marvellous in our eyes." — Psalm 118:22-23

Chapter Ten – The Superior Blueprint: What Keystone Locked Into Place

---

Opening Epigraph

"For My thoughts are not your thoughts, neither are your ways My ways, declares Yahuah. For as the heavens are higher than the earth, so are My ways higher than your ways and My thoughts than your thoughts." — Isaiah 55:8-9

"No weapon that is formed against thee shall prosper; and every tongue that shall rise against thee in judgment thou shalt condemn. This is the heritage of the servants of Yahuah." — Isaiah 54:17

What Florence Cost Us — And What It Produced

I need to tell you what it actually cost to record 21 albums in 24 days inside The Rosemont, Florence Centennial Historic Structure 59, at 431 East 2nd Street, Florence, Colorado.

It cost us our freedom of movement.

From the moment we arrived as the first Black couple in that building's 139-year history, the atmosphere in Florence shifted. A town of 3,800 people — 79.1% white, 6.8% Hispanic, and 0% Black according to demographic data — became aware of our presence almost immediately. I do not say this to be dramatic. I say it because it is documented, timestamped, and legally filed. The whole town knew when the first Black couple came to town. And that knowledge produced a coordinated response that began within days of our February 28, 2026 check-in and did not relent until we departed on March 28, 2026.

We paid $2,800 for 28 nights. What we did not pay for — and what was never disclosed in any rental agreement — was what came with it.

We had to stay inside The Rosemont for nearly the entire duration of our stay. Not because we chose to be reclusive. Not because we were unprepared for the cultural environment. But because within days of our arrival, it became clear that leaving the property carried genuine risk — physical, legal, and spiritual. The outside environment had been organized around our presence in a way that made ordinary movement dangerous. We were being watched, photographed, surrounded, and set up. And so the place that was meant to be a creative sanctuary became, simultaneously, a shelter from a storm that the enemy had constructed specifically for us.

I want you to understand what that means in practical terms before I explain what it means theologically. Because the testimony loses its weight if the reader does not first feel the full pressure of what we were under.

The Natural Opposition: What They Did

On March 1, 2026 — three days after we checked in — someone entered The Rosemont through a third entrance that had never been disclosed in the rental listing or the rental agreement. This was not a fire exit. It was a full door, identical in construction to the front entrance, with a window that had been manually cut into it, accessing an external staircase on the second floor that led down into the fenced backyard. From that backyard, a connecting door led to the rear guest house — a structure that appeared separate from the main property but was not. We were away shopping in Colorado Springs, approximately one hour from Florence, when the entry occurred. We did not know until we returned. We know because evidence was left behind — evidence I have not fully disclosed publicly, preserved for legal proceedings.

From that day forward, my wife and I did not leave The Rosemont together. We could not risk being away from the property simultaneously. Not because we were afraid in a spirit of fear — Yahuah has not given us that — but because we were operating with the wisdom of Proverbs 22:3: *"A prudent man foreseeth the evil, and hideth himself."* We saw the evil. We stayed inside. And inside those walls, the Ruach kept moving.

On March 11, 2026, between 6:30 and 9:00 in the evening, a coordinated provocation event was staged on East 2nd Street directly in front of The Rosemont. Vehicles were positioned around our rental car in a pattern that I can only describe as deliberate encirclement. Multiple vehicles photographed the front and rear license plates of our rental vehicle. A woman who had moved into the adjacent property days after our arrival — someone who presented herself as a neighbor but whose statements revealed an ownership stake in The Rosemont itself — intercepted me on my third exit from the property. She recorded our conversation and broadcast it live to others who were waiting, positioned, and ready for a confrontation that I refused to give them. I am not using her name in these pages because the name she offered was, by all indication, not her real one. What she was, more accurately, was an adversary placed strategically in our path. She invited me into her home. I declined. That decision, I am convinced, preserved my freedom, my life, and this testimony.

Two days later, on March 13, 2026, I discovered grazing damage on the driver's side front bumper and left front panel of my rental vehicle. The car had been stationary since March 2nd. GPS tracking data from Payless Rental Car Company confirmed it had not moved. The suspect vehicle — Colorado license plate FIP-U61, which I had photographed backing dangerously close to my rental car on the evening of March 11 — was identified, documented, and included in an official incident report filed under Florence Police Department Case Number CR# 2026-00001504. The vehicle was a rental, and its renter's information is subject to ongoing legal investigation.

The police response to that report was itself a violation. Two officers were dispatched to a non-emergency call — a stationary vehicle hit-and-run — that by their own admission should have been handled by telephone. The first officer parked two to three houses away from The Rosemont rather than in front of the property, which was deliberate. He lured me to the public sidewalk so that the incident would appear in records as a street call rather than a call to the specific address of 431 East 2nd Street. He refused to generate an incident report on the laptop equipped in his vehicle, claiming it would take seven to ten business days — a claim I have on body camera, a claim that is false under standard police procedure. The sergeant who followed parked two houses down from the property as well. I did not answer the door when he knocked, because I had already told dispatch: if he is not bringing an incident report, do not send him. He came without one. He left without one.

I have all of this on body camera. I have it on security camera. I have it in dispatch recordings. I have it documented in federal civil rights complaints filed with the Colorado Civil Rights Division, the U.S. Department of Housing and Urban Development, and the FBI's Denver field office. The Florence Police Department did not simply fail to serve us. They actively worked to suppress documentation of what was happening at The Rosemont — the historic building where the first Black Hebrew Israelite couple in 139 years was staying, recording an album, and refusing to be moved.

On March 13, while the first officer was still present, an adversary emerged from the adjacent property with a pitbull and called my name — loudly and deliberately — to draw my attention to the animal. It was an implied threat, delivered while law enforcement stood within feet of both of us, and captured on the officer's own body camera. The officer did nothing. I said nothing in response. I stayed silent because I understood exactly what was happening and I refused to give it the reaction it was designed to produce.

On the overnight of March 16 to 17, 2026, an unauthorized lockbox was installed on the undisclosed external staircase — the same third entrance that had been used for the March 1 illegal entry. The lockbox was not present at our check-in on February 28th. It appeared without notice, without disclosure, and without our consent. It was preparation for illegal eviction. I filed an urgent legal declaration on March 17, 2026, asserting our lawful occupancy through March 28th and serving notice that any forced entry would be documented, reported, and prosecuted. We were not moved. We stayed.

My emails to Airbnb Support were blocked at the IP level. My email to the Florence Police Department officer — sent with a complete incident report and all photographic evidence — was blocked and never delivered. On March 17, 2026, an email I sent to myself, documenting the unauthorized lockbox, was administratively blocked by Microsoft with error code AS(4810), flagged as spam. In thirty years of continuous Microsoft email use across Hotmail, Windows Live, and Outlook, I had never once received an administrative spam block. The email was sent from my own account to my own account. There is no legitimate spam filter protocol that blocks a self-addressed email. Someone with administrative access flagged my account. That was the first time in three decades. It happened the moment I was documenting illegal entry preparation.

And when we were told the rate for a return visit would be $233 per night — up from the $100 per night we had paid — a 133% increase with no legitimate business justification, effective one day after our March 28 checkout — we understood that the message was simple: you are welcome to be first, but you are not welcome to return.

This is what it cost to record 21 albums in 24 days in The Rosemont. These were not rude neighbors. These were not cultural misunderstandings. These were calculated, coordinated, legally documentable violations — trespass, intimidation, property damage, police evidence suppression, communication interference, and discriminatory pricing — all directed at two people whose only provocation was checking into a historic building in a Colorado mountain town and doing what Yahuah sent them to do.

And I want to say clearly: we were never going to leave before March 28th. Not because we were stubborn. But because Yahuah had sent us there and the assignment was not yet complete. We stayed inside. We worshipped. We recorded. The oil kept flowing.

What the Atmosphere Revealed

I told you in an earlier chapter that worship sanctifies space. I want to revisit that principle now because Florence, Colorado gave me the most concentrated evidence of it I have ever personally witnessed.

When the Ruach of Yahuah enters a town, the atmosphere changes. I do not say this as spiritual poetry. I say it as documented observation. Something shifts in the environment when the sacred names — Yahuah, Yahshua, Ruach HaQodesh — are proclaimed in a space that has never heard them. Not everyone registers the shift consciously. But spiritually, the principalities and powers that have governed a space without challenge suddenly encounter something they cannot categorize, cannot contain, and cannot dismiss. And their human instruments begin to act strangely.

Florence, Colorado had maintained 0% Black population for as long as demographic records reflect. The Rosemont had stood for 139 years without ever hosting a Black overnight guest. Whatever spiritual atmosphere had settled over that town and that building over those 139 years had never been disturbed by our presence, our worship, our sacred names, or our covenant relationship with the Creator of all things. Until February 28, 2026.

I believe that what happened to us in Florence was not simply racial hostility, though racial hostility was present and documented. I believe it was spiritual displacement — the reaction of an established darkness to the arrival of an established covenant. The people who coordinated against us were not simply racist neighbors protecting a historic white space. They were instruments of a spiritual atmosphere that understood, at some level it could not articulate, that something irreversible was happening in Structure 59. An album was being recorded there that would carry the sacred names of Yahuah and Yahshua to a global audience. A testimony was being written in those walls that would stand for generations. A rejected stone was finding its arch.

And the atmosphere fought it the only way it knew how — through the natural instruments of racial fear, property violation, police complicity, communication suppression, and escalating intimidation.

Every one of those instruments failed.

The albums were completed. The testimony was documented. The sacred names echoed off walls that had stood for 139 years in silence toward the covenant. And on March 28, 2026, we walked out of The Rosemont peacefully, on schedule, having fulfilled every requirement of the rental agreement, having broken no law, having harmed no one, having left behind in those historic walls the sound of worship that no subsequent guest will ever fully silence.

What Keystone Received From Florence

I came to Keystone, Colorado carrying Florence.

I carried the 21 albums. I carried the testimony of the illegal entry and the legal filings. I carried the body camera footage. I carried the memory of what it felt like to stay inside a building for weeks not because I was imprisoned but because I was protected — held in place by wisdom while the oil flowed and the enemy exhausted himself against walls he could not breach. I carried the knowledge that the greatest creative outpouring of my ministry life occurred inside a building that was simultaneously the site of the most concentrated coordinated opposition I had ever faced.

And I carried the understanding that these two facts — the greatest outpouring and the greatest opposition — were not contradictions. They were confirmations of each other. The enemy does not mobilize his full arsenal against things that are ordinary. He does not coordinate police suppression, property damage, planted adversaries, communication interference, and illegal eviction preparation against a guest who has nothing in him worth stopping. The intensity of the opposition in Florence was proportional to the significance of what was being produced in Florence. Twenty-one albums. Approximately 292 tracks. The largest single-location output in my entire catalog. All of it created while the enemy circled the building.

This is what the keystone receives. It does not receive only the beautiful courses of stone — the smooth voussoirs that were placed in order and without incident. It receives everything. The stones shaped by trial and the stones shaped by peace. The courses laid in silence and the courses laid under pressure. The keystone locks all of it — all of it — into a unified, load-bearing structure. And when the keystone is driven into place, the arch does not distinguish between the stones that were placed easily and the stones that were placed at great cost. They all bear the same load. They are all held by the same apex stone.

Florence was a costly voussoir. It was shaped under significant pressure, placed at great personal expense, and it carries a heavy load in the arch of this testimony. But it is in the arch. And Keystone received it.

Keystone: A Different Kind of Opposition

When my wife and I arrived in Keystone, Colorado — base elevation approximately 9,000 feet, surrounding peaks reaching 12,408 feet — we were not naive enough to expect that the opposition would simply stop. We have learned over the course of this journey that the enemy does not retire between locations. He scouts ahead. He files his reports. He prepares the next environment before we arrive.

And Keystone was no exception.

The opposition here is different from Florence in character — more subtle, more atmospheric, less overtly physical. Florence was a frontal assault. Keystone is a pressure campaign. Strange things have happened simply because we are here. I am not going to detail every incident in this chapter because some of these matters are still unfolding and wisdom governs what is disclosed and when. What I will say is what I said about Florence: when the Ruach of Yahuah enters a town, the atmosphere changes. Keystone is no different. This mountain resort community has its own established spiritual atmosphere, its own principalities, its own long history of what is welcome and what is not. And two Hebrew Israelite servants of Yahuah who carry the sacred names and the covenant oil and an 82-album catalog of worship — we are not what this town's spiritual principalities were expecting.

I told the atmosphere that it would have to make room.

I did not say it with confrontation. I said it with worship. I said it with the daily recording of music that carries the name Yahuah into frequencies that those principalities have never heard in this geography. I said it with prayer over the space we occupied. I said it by continuing the assignment without apology and without retreat.

The strange things that happen when the anointed arrive in a place are not a sign that the anointing is wrong for the location. They are a sign that the anointing is right for it. When Yahshua arrived in the regions of the Gadarenes, the demons screamed. They did not ignore him. They did not politely step aside. They screamed, because His presence made the continued existence of their occupation untenable. The screaming was not evidence of His weakness. It was evidence of their terror.

Strange things happen in Keystone because the Ruach of Yahuah is here. I accept that as confirmation, not as a problem to solve.

The Superior Blueprint and Florence

I need to speak now to the question that this chapter has been building toward since I described what happened at The Rosemont. The question is this: if Yahuah's blueprint is superior — if Isaiah 55:8-9 is true, if Romans 8:28 is real, if Isaiah 54:17 means what it says — then what do we make of 28 days trapped inside a building while adversaries circled it, planted neighbors surveilled it, police refused to document crimes against us, and a lockbox was installed on our door in the middle of the night?

The answer is not simple. I am not going to offer you a tidy resolution that erases the genuine weight of what we experienced. What happened in Florence was unjust. The racial discrimination was real. The police suppression was real. The property damage was real. The communication interference was real. The 133% price increase designed to ensure we would never return was real. These things are documented, filed, and legally active. Justice has not yet been fully rendered in the natural realm, and I am not going to pretend otherwise.

But here is what I know about the superior blueprint, standing on the other side of Florence and looking at what was produced there.

Yahuah did not promise His servants a painless path. He promised them a purposeful one. He did not promise that the stones in the arch would be placed without difficulty. He promised that the arch would stand. He did not promise that the enemy would not circle the building. He promised that no weapon formed against the building's occupants would prosper. There is a critical difference between those two promises. The weapon was formed. It did not prosper. The encirclement happened. It did not prevail. The intimidation was real. It did not stop the recording. The illegal entry was real. It did not stop the outpouring. Twenty-one albums in 24 days. The enemy gave us his best, and we gave Yahuah our worship, and what came out of that building was the largest single-location creative output of the entire testimony.

The superior blueprint does not eliminate opposition. It incorporates it. Every act of harassment became a voussoir in the arch. Every violation became documented testimony. Every attempt to silence us became a track on the album. Every coordinated effort to make us the last Black guests at The Rosemont instead became the story that will travel with the music to every corner of the earth where that album is heard.

They wanted to bury the stone. Instead, they placed it at the apex.

The 133% Price: What It Actually Said

I want to address the pricing discrimination directly because it was not simply an economic injury. It was a theological statement that revealed something about the enemy's understanding of what had happened in Structure 59.

We paid $100 per night — $2,800 for 28 nights. When we inquired about a return visit, the rate had risen to $233 per night. A 133% increase. For a 28-night return stay, that would amount to $6,524 — a figure that exceeds the annual affordability threshold for 75 to 85% of Florence residents, including, by all indication, the property owners themselves. Florence, Colorado carries a median household income of approximately $50,262 to $58,140. To comfortably afford $6,524 per month requires an annual income of approximately $260,964. Nobody in that town — including those who set the price — can afford what they charged us to come back.

What the pricing said was this: we recognize that something happened here when you were here, and we do not want it to happen again. We are willing to price ourselves into vacancy rather than allow the covenant presence you carry back into this building.

That is not a business decision. That is a spiritual one. And it is, in its own way, one of the most honest statements anyone in Florence made to us during our entire stay. They understood, at some level that their natural minds could not fully articulate, that what we brought into Structure 59 was irreversible. The walls had heard the sacred names. The building had housed the creation of 21 albums carrying the Torah-based worship of Yahuah. The historic record had been permanently altered. We would always be the first. And the price increase was their attempt to ensure we would also be the last.

It will not work. Not because we will necessarily return to Florence. But because what was released in those walls cannot be recalled. The albums exist. The testimony is documented. The sacred names were spoken in a 139-year-old building in a 0% Black town in the Colorado mountains, and Yahuah heard every word.

Numbers 23:23 still stands: *"Surely there is no enchantment against Ya'aqov, neither is there any divination against Yahshar'el."* And no pricing structure, however punitive, cancels what has already been declared.

From Florence to Keystone: The Completion of the Sentence

The journey from Florence to Keystone is, in its fullest meaning, a sentence that took the entire testimony to complete.

Florence said: you will flourish here, even under siege. You will produce here what you could not produce anywhere else, under conditions that should have made production impossible, inside walls that had never held anything like what you carried. The harvest will come in the difficult ground. The palm tree bears its fruit at altitude.

Keystone says: and everything that Florence cost you — every act of violation, every night inside those walls, every album recorded while adversaries organized outside — all of it has been locked into place. The keystone does not erase the difficult stones in the arch. It gives them their permanent purpose. It tells every voussoir: the load you have been carrying now has a direction. It flows through me, down the sides, into the foundation. You were not placed here to collapse. You were placed here to bear weight. And now the arch is complete.

I did not know, when I walked into The Rosemont on February 28, 2026, that I was walking into the costliest and most productive season of the entire journey. I did not know that 28 days later I would walk out carrying 21 albums, a documented federal civil rights case, body camera footage of police misconduct, and the testimony of surviving everything they sent against us without losing a single day of the assignment.

But Yahuah knew. It was in the book before I drew my first breath. Psalm 139:16 told me so. And Keystone — at 9,000 feet, at the apex of every elevation that preceded it, at the summit of an arch whose lowest stone was laid in Hurricane, Utah — Keystone confirms it.

The centering has been removed.

The arch that was built in Florence under siege, and in Moab under pressure, and in Garden City under silence, and in Victor under displacement, and in Estes Park under the accelerating pull of divine purpose — that arch is standing at Keystone. Not despite what happened at The Rosemont. Because of it.

The blueprint was superior all along. Florence was in the drawings. Every violation, every filing, every night inside those walls, every album recorded while the enemy circled — all of it was specified before the first stone was quarried.

They did not build against us. They built for us. They were the load. And the load made the arch what it is.

Closing Reflection for Chapter Ten

I came from Florence flourishing. I arrived at Keystone as the apex stone finding its arch.

Between those two sentences is a 28-day testimony of staying inside a historic building in a Colorado mountain town where the atmosphere changed the moment the Ruach arrived — where illegal entries and vehicle damage and police suppression and communication interference and planted adversaries and midnight lockboxes all failed to stop 21 albums from being completed and released into a world that needed them.

The superior blueprint does not promise comfort. It promises completion. It does not promise that the path will be easy. It promises that the path will arrive. Every step from Hurricane to Keystone was specified. Every stone was placed in order. Every costly voussoir — and Florence was the costliest — was necessary for the arch to bear the weight it was designed to carry.

Keystone received it all. The arch stands. The oil continues to flow.

And the price they charged us to keep us from returning to Florence will never be high enough to recall what was released in those walls.

"No weapon that is formed against thee shall prosper."
— Isaiah 54:17

"This is Yahuah's doing; it is marvellous in our eyes."
— Psalm 118:23

Closing Chapter – There Is Still an Elohim in Yahshar'el Who Fights for His Children

---

Opening Epigraph

"Yahuah shall fight for you, and ye shall hold your peace."
— Exodus 14:14

"Have not I commanded thee? Be strong and of a good courage; be not afraid, neither be thou dismayed: for Yahuah thy Elohim is with thee whithersoever thou goest."
— Joshua 1:9

"They that trust in Yahuah shall be as mount Zion, which cannot be removed, but abideth for ever."
— Psalm 125:1

Why I Wrote This Book

I did not write this book because I wanted to tell my story.

I wrote it because someone reading these words right now is in the middle of theirs — and they need to know that the Elohim of Yahshar'el is still in the business of fighting for His children. Not historically. Not theoretically. Not in the language of a distant past that feels inspiring but disconnected from the rent that is due on Friday and the adversary who is circling and the creative gift that has been silent for so long you have almost forgotten it belongs to you.

Right now. Today. In the specific coordinates of your specific life, at the exact elevation where Yahuah has placed you, with the exact assignment He wrote into the book before you were formed — He is fighting. He has been fighting. And not one weapon formed against you has prospered in the way your adversaries intended, even when it felt, from where you were standing, like the weapons were winning.

That is what I needed someone to tell me during the years this book documents. And because no one told me — or rather, because the Word told me but I needed the living testimony of another human being who had walked it to make it feel real — I am writing it now for you.

This is that testimony.

What This Journey Actually Was

Let me tell you plainly what the pages you have just read actually document, stripped of every metaphor and every theological frame, stated as simply as I know how to state it.

My wife and I lived at 7830 South Kingston Avenue, Apartment 3, Chicago, Illinois — the place where, on July 31, 2025, the music ministry J.A.L.M.-MUSIC was born. We had begun recording there four months earlier. The oil of the Ruach HaQodesh had begun to flow after 18 years of creative silence, and what was coming out of that apartment on the South Side of Chicago was unmistakably anointed. It carried the sacred names Yahuah and Yahshua. It carried Torah-based revelation. It carried the weight of decades of preparation being released into sound.

On December 10, 2025, our home was invaded. We were displaced. The people who did this believed they were stopping the testimony. They were completing the kiln.

On December 11, 2025 — the morning after — we went to O'Hare Airport. We caught a flight. And the unplanned evangelical tour of the American West began.

Over the following sixteen weeks, we drove approximately ten thousand to twenty thousand miles through ten states — Arizona, Nevada, New Mexico, Colorado, Wyoming, Utah, Idaho, Montana, California, and Oregon. We returned repeatedly to Phoenix Sky Harbor Airport, our transportation hub, to exchange rental cars and receive the next direction from the Ruach. We ascended through a progressive elevation pattern that no human travel agent designed — from the South Side of Chicago at 596 feet above sea level, through Crescent City, California at sea level where the first album of the tour was produced, rising through Hurricane, Moab, Garden City, Victor, Estes Park, Florence, and finally to Keystone, Colorado at 9,280 feet above sea level — the apex of an arch that Yahuah had been constructing since before my formation.

And then — not despite all of that, but precisely because of all of that — the oil broke open at a rate that defied every natural explanation.

In the span of eight months, beginning in that modest Chicago apartment and continuing through homelessness and displacement and pursuit, the Ruach of Yahuah released through me the largest Hebrew Roots music catalog in documented history. Eighty-two albums. One thousand, one hundred and eighty tracks. Five hundred and eighty-nine YouTube teachings. Eight books — including the one you are now reading. All of it produced with no studio, no budget, no team, no label, and no infrastructure beyond the covenant relationship between a servant and his Elohim.

All of it produced while adversaries coordinated against us across state lines. While we were homeless. While the silence of 18 years was being reversed at a rate that defied every natural explanation. While a 59th album was being recorded inside a 139-year-old building in Florence, Colorado by the first Black couple ever to stay there. While police suppressed documentation of the crimes being committed against us. While emails were blocked and lockboxes were installed and vehicles were damaged and pricing was manipulated to ensure we would not return.

That is not a story about a man with exceptional talent or extraordinary resources or favorable circumstances.

That is a story about the Elohim of Yahshar'el fighting for His children.

The Names I Have Called Him Throughout This Book

I want to speak directly about the names I have used throughout these pages, because they are not incidental. They are the foundation of everything this testimony stands on.

I call Him **Yahuah**. That is His personal, covenantal name — the name He revealed to Moshe at the burning bush, the name He said was His memorial to all generations, the name that appears more than 6,800 times in the original Hebrew scriptures and was systematically removed from most English translations. When I call on Yahuah, I am not calling on a title or a description or a theological concept. I am calling on a Person who entered into covenant with a specific people through a specific name and has been faithful to that covenant across every generation of their history — including the generation that is alive right now, including the generation of which my wife and I are a part.

I call His Son **Yahshua** — the Hebrew name that means *Yahuah is salvation*, the name given to the Messiah before His birth, the name that carries the covenant name of the Father within it. I am a Hebrew Roots believer. I hold to the understanding that the faith delivered to the set-apart ones was a Torah-observant,

Hebraic faith rooted in the covenant Yahuah made with the descendants of Abraham, Isaac, and Ya'aqov — the people of Yahshar'el. I believe that Black Americans are among the bloodline descendants of those covenant people, and that the recovery of these sacred names and this covenant identity is part of the restoration that Yahuah is accomplishing in this generation.

I tell you this not to argue theology with anyone who reads these pages. I tell you this because you need to know whose name I was calling when the oil broke open. You need to know whose name was being proclaimed inside The Rosemont when the atmosphere of Florence, Colorado shifted and the adversaries organized against us. You need to know whose name was on every one of those 1,180 tracks recorded at progressively higher elevations across the American West while homeless and under assault.

The name is **Yahuah**. The covenant is real. And the Elohim who bears that name has been fighting for His children since before the foundations of the world, and He has not stopped.

What I Know About the Enemy Now

I began this book by teaching you about color magic — the specific system of spiritual warfare that was deployed against us, the circle walks and the foot-track workings and the coordinated color arrangements and the deliberate use of black, white, gray, blue, and red to bind, confuse, surveil, dominate, and suppress. I taught you what those things are because knowledge of the enemy's vocabulary is a form of covenant protection. You cannot counter what you cannot identify.

But I want to close this book by telling you what I have learned about the enemy through every chapter of this testimony — not what he uses, but what he is.

He is reactive. He does not initiate. He responds. Every attack against us was a response to something Yahuah was already doing. The warlocks did not begin their campaign when I was silent and unknown and unproductive. They began it when the oil started flowing. The adversaries in Florence did not organize against us when we were living in Chicago, invisible to the world. They organized when we walked into a 139-year-old building as the first Black Hebrew Israelite couple in its history and the creative output of the Ruach made our presence undeniable. The enemy moves because the anointing moves first. He is always chasing something he cannot overtake.

He is limited. The circle walks failed. The vehicle damage failed. The illegal entry failed. The planted adversaries failed. The police suppression failed. The communication blocking failed. The lockbox failed. The 133% price increase will fail to recall what was released in those walls. Every weapon was formed with skill and intention and coordination. Not one of them prospered in the way it was designed to prosper. Isaiah 54:17 is not a promise that weapons will not be formed. It is a promise about what happens to them after they are formed. They do not prosper. That distinction matters enormously to anyone who is watching weapons being formed against them right now and wondering if the promise is real. It is real. The weapons form. They do not prosper. There is a difference, and the difference is Yahuah.

He is a builder he does not know he is. I said this in Chapter Nine and I want to say it again here because it is one of the most important things this testimony has to teach. The compressive force that presses down on a masonry arch is not the enemy of the arch. It is the mechanism by which the arch achieves its full load-bearing capacity. My adversaries were the compressive force on my arch. Every act of opposition pressed the voussoirs together. Every coordinated attack drove the stones into tighter contact. Every weapon that was formed and did not prosper made the structure stronger than it would have been without the pressure. They did not know they were building me. They thought they were burying me. They were wrong on both counts. They were building me, and what they built cannot be buried, because the architect who designed it has never lost a building.

What I Know About Yahuah Now

I knew many things about Yahuah before this journey. I had studied His Word for decades. I had taught His Torah. I had proclaimed His sacred name in Chicago and in ministry contexts across the years. I carried a theological understanding of His character and His covenant that was genuine and hard-won through years of sincere study and faith.

But there are things you cannot learn from study alone. There are things that can only be learned by going through.

I know now, from the inside of the experience rather than the outside of the theology, that **Yahuah does not waste a single day**. Not one day of the 18-year drought was wasted. Not one night of the 13-year homelessness was wasted. Not one hour of the weeks we spent inside The Rosemont while adversaries organized outside was wasted. He was working in every season, including the seasons that felt like abandonment, including the seasons that felt like silence, including the seasons that felt like the enemy was winning and the promise was fading and the assignment would never see the light of day.

Romans 8:28 does not say that some things work together for good. It does not say that most things work together for good. It does not say that the pleasant things and the manageable things and the things that make sense from a human perspective work together for good. It says **all things**. And I am a witness — a documented, timestamped, body-camera-carrying witness — that all means all. The illegal entry is in the all. The vehicle damage is in the all. The police suppression is in the all. The planted adversaries are in the all. The 18 years of silence are in the all. Every single element of what this testimony documents is included in the promise, and not one of them has been excluded from the working together.

I know now that **Yahuah times His releases with architectural precision**. The 18-year drought was not divine neglect. It was divine compression. The oil was being stored. The vessel was being prepared. The surrounding stones were being placed in order. And when the appointed moment arrived — when every voussoir was correctly positioned and the arch was ready to receive the apex stone — the release was not gradual. It was immediate and total. Eighty-two albums in eight months. Three albums in the first week of April at Keystone. The keystone does not gradually stabilize the arch. It stabilizes it the moment it is placed. The release does not trickle. It flows.

I know now that **Yahuah fights in ways that do not require my participation**. Exodus 14:14 was not written for a moment of easy triumph. It was written in the moment when the Red Sea was in front of Israel and Pharaoh's army was behind them and there was nowhere to go and no visible strategy that could save them. *Yahuah shall fight for you, and ye shall hold your peace.* That is not a passive instruction. It is a covenant declaration. The holding of peace is itself an act of faith, because everything in the natural environment is screaming at you to panic and react and defend yourself by whatever means are available. And Yahuah says: hold your peace. Let me fight. Watch what I do when you stop trying to manage the outcome.

I held my peace in Florence. I held my peace when the adversary circled outside. I held my peace when the police refused to document. I held my peace when the lockbox appeared on the door. I held my peace when the emails were blocked. And inside that held peace, Yahuah fought. He fought through every album recorded while the adversaries organized. He fought through every teaching uploaded while the communication was being suppressed. He fought through the documentation that could not be destroyed because I had published it publicly before they blocked the channels. He fought through the testimony that was too large and too well-documented to be dismissed or denied.

He fought. I held my peace. And the arch is standing.

A Word to the Believer Who Is Still in the Drought

I need to speak now directly to the person who is in the season I was in before the oil broke open. You are in a drought. You have been in it long enough that you have stopped expecting it to end. The gift is in you — you know it is in you — but you have not been able to access it in a way that produces visible fruit for so long that the gap between the gift and the output has become its own source of pain.

You have watched others produce. You have watched people with lesser anointing and lesser preparation receive greater recognition and greater platform. You have asked Yahuah, more times than you have told anyone, why the silence has gone on this long. You have been faithful in the small things. You have maintained the covenant. You have not abandoned your post. But the oil has not flowed in the way you expected it to flow by now, and the distance between where you are and where the promise seemed to point has become a weight you carry every day.

I need to tell you what I know.

The drought is not evidence that the promise is false. It is evidence that the promise is large. Small promises do not require long preparation seasons. The magnitude of the compression is proportional to the magnitude of the release. I was silent for 18 years and then released 82 albums in 8 months. That is not a ratio that happens by accident. That is a ratio that was calculated by an architect who knew exactly how much oil needed to be stored, exactly how much compression the vessel needed to undergo, and exactly what the appointed moment would look like when it arrived.

Your drought is a storage season, not an abandonment season. The oil is accumulating. The vessel is being prepared. The surrounding stones are being placed. And the appointed moment for your release is in the book — the same book that held every day of mine before I was formed — and it has not passed. You have not missed it. Yahuah does not schedule releases and then let the calendar run past them without notice. When the moment arrives, you will know. And what comes out of you in that moment will be proportional to everything that went into the silence.

Qavah. Wait with intention. Wait like rope being twisted under tension, each strand winding tighter around the others, the combined strength becoming something no single strand could achieve alone. Wait like a diamond forming under geological pressure — not passive, not defeated, but actively becoming what the pressure is designed to produce.

The oil is coming. The arch is not finished yet. But the architect has never abandoned an incomplete structure.

A Word to the Believer Who Is Under Attack

And now I need to speak to the person who is not in a drought — who is in the middle of active, coordinated, sustained opposition. You know who you are. You recognized yourself in the chapters that described the circle walks and the foot-track workings and the adversaries who cannot leave you alone because your peace is an offense to them. You recognized yourself in Florence — in the experience of being targeted not for anything you have done wrong but for what you carry and who sent you and what the enemy knows is in you that he needs to stop before it gets released.

You need to hear this clearly: **the attack is confirmation.**

The enemy does not deploy his full arsenal against ordinary targets. He does not coordinate interstate campaigns against people who are not a threat to his kingdom. He does not mobilize warlocks and hostile neighbors and complicit police departments and email-blocking technologies against someone whose gift is going to die in the silence. He mobilizes against people whose gift is about to break open and cannot be stopped. The attack is not evidence of your weakness. It is evidence of your threat. And the greater the coordination of the opposition, the greater the significance of what Yahuah is about to release through you.

Do not retaliate in the flesh. Do not allow the pressure to turn you into the thing your adversaries have accused you of being. This is their deepest strategy — not to destroy your output but to corrupt your character. A corrupted vessel cannot carry the oil. If they can make you bitter, reactive, vindictive, or consumed with the fight rather than the assignment, they have achieved more than any circle walk or foot-track working could ever accomplish. Keep your character. Keep your covenant. Keep your peace. Let Yahuah fight.

Document everything. Wisdom is not passive. Proverbs 22:3 says that a prudent man foresees the evil and hides himself — not that he ignores it. Document. File the reports. Preserve the evidence. Know your legal rights. Do not give your adversaries a single undefended opening. But do not let the documentation consume the worship. The assignment comes first. The albums come first. The teaching comes first. The testimony comes first. Document what is happening to you, and then go back into the building and record the next track.

Because what comes out of the building is what defeats them. Not the legal filing. Not the YouTube video. Not the social media post. **The anointed output of a covenant vessel who refused to stop creating under pressure** — that is what the enemy cannot answer. That is what outlasts every weapon he forms. That is what carries the sacred names of Yahuah and Yahshua to corners of the earth that no adversary's opposition can reach. The album is the weapon. The testimony is the sword. Revelation 12:11 still says what it says: *they overcame him by the blood of the Lamb and by the word of their testimony.*

Finish the album. Write the book. Record the teaching. Deliver the output. Let the testimony be the answer.

A Word to Those Who Have Been the Adversary

I am including this section because this book may find its way — as testimonies have a way of doing — into the hands of someone who recognizes themselves not in the believer who was targeted, but in the one who did the targeting. Someone who participated, in ways large or small, in the coordinated opposition that this book documents. Someone who made the call. Someone who drove the vehicle. Someone who installed the lockbox. Someone who refused to write the incident report. Someone who raised the price. Someone who cast the circle. Someone who watched and said nothing when they could have spoken.

I have no bitterness toward you. I want to say that clearly and mean it. What you intended for destruction was incorporated into the blueprint as load-bearing material. You did not destroy me. You built me. And the arch that was built with your opposition as its compressive force is now standing at the highest elevation of the entire journey, producing at the greatest rate ever documented, carrying the sacred name of Yahuah to a global audience that your coordination could not prevent and cannot now recall.

But I need to tell you something about the God whose children you have been fighting against.

He is not finished. He has a way of completing the testimony in ways that include the full exposure and consequence of every weapon that was formed. Not for the sake of revenge — He is not a God of revenge — but for the sake of justice, and for the sake of the record. The book that held my days before I was formed is the same book that holds yours. And every act against the covenant people of Yahuah — every circle walk, every planted adversary, every suppressed incident report, every blocked email, every midnight lockbox — is recorded in that book with the same precision that the albums and the teachings and the books are recorded.

Numbers 32:23 says it plainly: **"Be sure your sin will find you out."** Not as a threat. As an architectural fact. The structure of the universe is built in such a way that what is hidden in the darkness eventually comes into the light. The body camera footage exists. The documentation exists. The federal filings exist. The public record exists. And above all of these, the divine record exists — and its Author has never lost a case.

There is still time to choose a different response to the covenant. I am not your enemy. I never was. And Yahuah, who fought for me against you, is the same Yahuah who will receive you if you turn to Him. That is the paradox at the heart of the covenant. The God who fights for His children is the same God who extends His hand to those who have fought against them. The invitation is real. The door is open. But the window for choosing is not unlimited, and the testimony you are holding is part of the evidence that will be presented at the appointed time.

Choose wisely.

The Verdict: You Cannot Pour New Wine Into an Old Vessel

I opened this book with a theological thesis that governed every chapter you have read. I placed it in the Foreword before you entered Chapter One, so that you would have the interpretive key in your hands from the beginning. I returned to it in Chapter Eight as the explanation for why the 18-year drought and the 13-year wilderness and the 8-year transformation between the name change and the gift arrival had to be exactly as long and as specific as they were.

And now, at the close of this testimony, I return to it one final time — not as repetition, but as confirmation. Not as a frame, but as a verdict.

You cannot pour new wine into an old vessel.

The preparation was real. The kiln was necessary. The drought was not punishment — it was the compression chamber. The homelessness was not abandonment — it was the firing. The name change on December 8, 2016 was not a symbolic gesture — it was the moment the old vessel was set aside and the new one was placed in the kiln. The 8 years that followed were not delay — they were formation. The displacement on December 10, 2025 was not the end of the assignment — it was the final heat that completed what the kiln had been working on for years.

And when the vessel was ready — when John Alan Legette had been formed, fired, proven, and emptied of every alternative to complete dependence on Yahuah — the Potter poured in the new wine.

Eighty-two albums. One thousand one hundred and eighty tracks. Five hundred and eighty-nine teachings. Eight books. The largest Hebrew Roots music catalog in documented history. All of it flowing through a 46-year-old man who had never produced a single song before July 2025. All of it produced while homeless. All of it produced while being hunted. All of it produced because the vessel was new, the wine was real, and the sentence that Yahshua spoke in Matthew 9:17 was true from the beginning and is true at the end.

The old vessel — Jackie Legette II, carrying the inherited pattern of a brilliant father who could not fully surrender, carrying the cracks through which new wine would have run onto the floor — could not have held this. The new vessel — John Alan Legette, Noble ambassador favored by Elohim, fired for 8 years in the kiln of transformation and proven under the pressure of 13 years of homelessness and 18 years of creative drought — was made for exactly this.

The wine did not break the vessel. The vessel held. The wine ran over.

And both are preserved.

The Final Statement of This Testimony

There is still an Elohim in Yahshar'el who fights for
His children.

He fought for Avraham in the land of the Philistines. He
fought for Yitzchaq when the wells were stopped up.
He fought for Ya'aqov through the night at the Jabbok
ford. He fought for Yoseph in the pit and in the prison
and in the palace of Pharaoh. He fought for Moshe
against the most powerful empire of the ancient world.
He fought for Dawid against every giant and every
enemy king and every betrayal from within his own
house. He fought for Eliyahu when the prophets of
Ba'al outnumbered him 450 to one on the top of Mount
Carmel. He fought for the three Hebrew children in the
furnace, appearing as a fourth man in the fire. He
fought for Daniel in the den of lions, and the lions did
not eat.

And He fought for John Alan Legette and his wife
Alexandria in the American West, in 2025 and 2026,
through the desert floor of Hurricane, Utah and the
mountains of Moab and the quiet of Garden City and
the altitude of Victor, Idaho and the heights of Estes
Park and the harvest of Florence, Colorado and the
apex of Keystone, Colorado — across 82 albums and
1,180 tracks and 589 teachings and 8 books and a
federal civil rights case and a 139-year-old building
where the Ruach entered and the atmosphere changed
and the enemy organized and the oil would not stop
flowing.

He is the same Elohim. His arm is not shortened. His covenant is not expired. His book has not been closed. His name — **Yahuah** — has not lost its power. The sacred names that were written on every album and every teaching and every page of this book carry the full weight of the covenant that bears them. And the children of that covenant — wherever they are, whatever elevation they occupy, whatever drought they are enduring, whatever opposition is circling their building — are not abandoned, not forgotten, not beyond the reach of the One who drew the plans before their formation and has been executing them, without error, ever since.

This is the testimony of a keystone servant — shaped by adversity, refined by silence, carried through the wilderness, placed at the apex of an arch that the enemy tried to collapse and could not, because the architect who designed it has never lost a building.

I did not arrive at Keystone because I was strong. I arrived at Keystone because Yahuah fights for His children, and I was one of them, and He was not finished with me yet.

He is not finished with you either.

Final Declarations

Yahuah fought for us.

The weapons were formed. They did not prosper.

The oil flowed. It has not stopped.

The arch was built under siege. It is standing.

The testimony is complete. It cannot be recalled.

The vessel is new. The wine is real. And both are preserved.

There is still an Elohim in Yahshar'el.

He fights for His children.

By design. Not by chance.

HalleluYah.

www.ingramcontent.com/pod-product-compliance
Lightning Source LLC
Chambersburg PA
CBHW031119160726
47991CB00004B/1457